Music
Cities

Concept and editorial care
Balthazar Pagani

Graphic design and layout
Bebung

Iconographic research
Rachele Adda

Music Cities

**The Capitals and Places
of Music Geography**

Edited by Guia Cortassa

whitestar˙

Contents

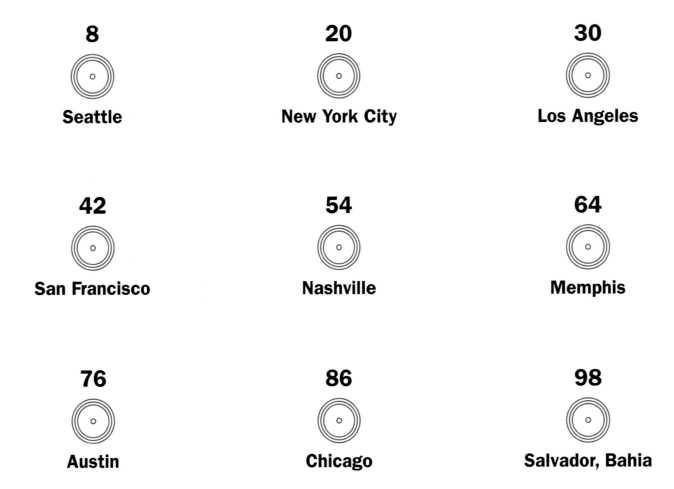

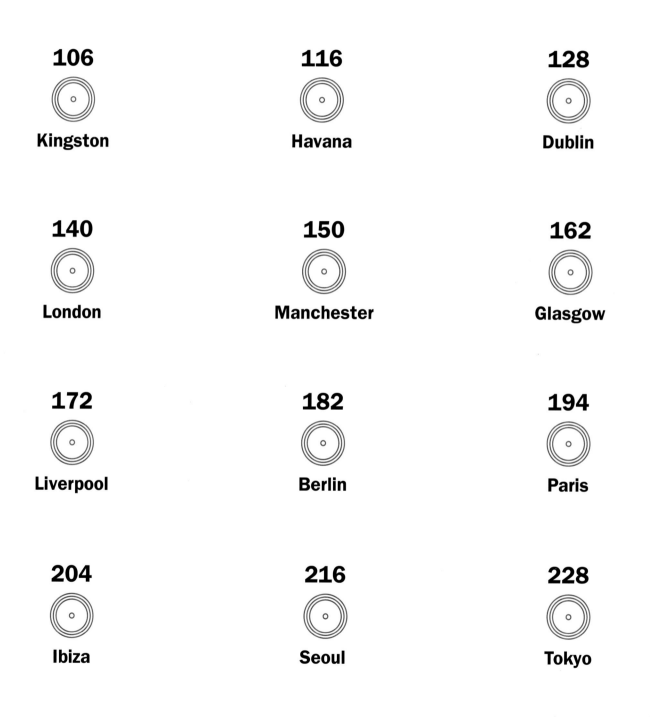

106
Kingston

116
Havana

128
Dublin

140
London

150
Manchester

162
Glasgow

172
Liverpool

182
Berlin

194
Paris

204
Ibiza

216
Seoul

228
Tokyo

The Geography of Revolutions of Sound

**This book is not an encyclopedia or a travel guide.
It might seem like an atlas, but it's not quite that either.
This book is a patchwork collection. It is the story of those
times when a city found itself at center stage of a breaking point
or moment of change in the history of twentieth- and twenty-
first-century music. There are places that hosted very brief
experiences, which left such a deep mark that they still resonate
in music today, and others that, as the decades passed, never
ceased to be incubators of talent and innovation, standing as
veritable beacons for record producers, musicians, and fans.**

In these pages, we move seamlessly from recounting the lives of individual people to chroni-
cling cultural tides that influenced entire nations, from exploring historical locales to telling
the legends of others, because the spark that ignites history can come from the dream of a
single girl singing in a dank old cellar as much as it can from the collective feeling of an entire
population. Some might not find the names they expected to read in a specific chapter, and
others will discover ones they have never heard of. Far from any encyclopedic or completist
afflatus, without any chronological or spatial constraints, the purpose of this book is to tell
when and how some of the cities we have come to recognize as industry hubs were put on
the map of "popular" Western music history.

Music, like every city, is an experience to be lived, to be felt vibrating in your bones, resonating in every part of your body. Every city, like music, is constantly changing, involved in a continuous process of stratification that sprouts new seeds on the remnants of what came before, a creative and cultural hummus that serves as fertile ground for new experimentation. Maps are used to discover what the present has done to the places of history and how the past has shaped neighborhoods and entire cities of the present day. Exploring urban space adds a concrete dimension to the most ephemeral and evanescent art form man has ever created: music. Yet above all, it is capable of evoking even long-gone memories and feelings.

And what could be better than being carried away by a city's maze of streets, sidewalks, alleys, and ups and downs, listening to its sound, the sound that has made it unique and unmistakable, and letting your mind and thoughts indulge in an all-encompassing synesthesia? Between large immersive spaces and clubs so small they are almost impossible to find, house-museums and stadium-sized discos, the journey mapped out on these pages is studded with well-known names and the illustrious unknown, unimaginable landmarks, and moments to be experienced and relived with your eyes and ears.

So turn up the volume and head out. Happy reading.

Seattle

Seattle's name is inextricably linked to the 1990s, when the explosion first of grunge and later the disruptiveness of the no-global movements brought it to global prominence. Its location, seemingly peripheral to US spheres of influence, actually made it fertile ground for the birth and establishment of major alternative cultural movements. Seattle, in fact, has a long-standing musical tradition that started at the dawn of the twentieth century.

In the early twentieth century, before jazz took over and when movies were still new, the most popular form of entertainment in the United States was vaudeville, a genre likened to variety theater made up of shows consisting of comedy numbers, burlesque, music, and dance. Evening outings were considered social events, and cities glittered with the majestic architecture of theaters that brought the new American dream to life. Seattle was no exception, and its streets sparkled under the twinkling lights of the hall catwalks. Over time, many of these cathedrals of entertainment were torn down, but three remain today: the Moore, the oldest, which retains its original furnishings from 1907; the 5th Avenue Theatre, built in 1926, magnificent in its interior inspired by Beijing's Forbidden City and still the city's main venue for musical performances; and finally the Paramount, built in 1928 and restored in 1995, where Pink Floyd, Queen, and Nirvana played, as well as Madonna, who performed her first three concerts there in 1985.

The 1920s saw a flourishing jazz scene, which had become the predominant genre throughout the United States. Between 1918 and 1951, an endless line of clubs and nightclubs lined Jackson Street, where it was possible to find hot jazz jams at all hours of the day and night, someone to dance with, and, most importantly, bootleg alcohol. Ray Charles, Quincy Jones, and Ernestine Anderson saw their careers take off in these smoky clubs. From the stage of the Black and Tan Club, the longest-running club in the area, came Duke Ellington and Charlie Parker. In 1947, seventeen-year-old Ray Charles managed to become a regular musician, along with Garcia McKee, at the Black Elks Club, where he soon met an even younger Quincy Jones, resulting in an extraordinary partnership.

The focus shifted from jazz to rock in the 1960s, which in the Pacific Northwest found its most extreme expression, one that embodied everything that parents of the time considered "dangerous" about rock and roll.

It was during this period that a young guitarist took his first steps before enlisting in the army, debuting in 1960 with an anonymous band at the Jaffe Room at Temple De Hirsch. The name of the boy, who in 1968 would receive the keys to the city in recognition of his musical career, was Johnny Allen Hendrix, but soon everyone would know him simply as Jimi Hendrix.

In 1979, Bruce Pavitt, a student at Evergreen State College in Olympia, founded *Subterranean Pop*, a fanzine devoted to the world of music and independent labels, distributed in photocopied issues. The success of its publication led him, after only four issues, to alternate paper issues with music cassettes featuring compilations of underground bands. In 1986, having relocated from Olympia to Seattle, with the help of Jonathan Poneman, Pavitt turned the publishing project, which had since shortened its name, into a record company, giving birth to Sub Pop Records. The label quickly became the go-to label for the local alternative scene, and bands such as Green River and Mudhoney began to appear on its roster. In its first two years, it succeeded in shaping the "Seattle sound," which thanks to a word used in the press release for Green River's first record, would become known worldwide as "grunge." The sounds, which harken back to punk and heavy metal, are dirty and distorted; the songs speak of social alienation, insecurity, isolation, addiction, trauma, and the desire for freedom; all the glamour of pop is drowned in a sea of nihilism and sarcasm.

The grunge scene orbited around the Belltown neighborhood, a former industrial area turned artist hangout. The Black Dog Forge was a hot spot, and Pearl Jam and Soundgarden rehearsed in its basement. Evenings at the Crocodile Cafe hosted concerts and secret shows, and in 1997, Death Cab for Cutie debuted there. The University of Washington radio station, then called KCMU (now KEXP), was a cultural stronghold, and members of grunge bands passed through its studio daily for DJ sets and interviews.

The Seattle sound reached its most successful moment in 1991 with the release of Nirvana's *Nevermind*, Pearl Jam's *Ten*, Soundgarden's *Badmotorfinger*, and Mudhoney's *Every Good Boy Deserves Fudge*, but its flame was destined to extinguish soon; Kurt Cobain, leader of Nirvana, died of a self-inflicted gunshot wound on April 5, 1994. Five days later, more than 7,000

The 5th Avenue Theatre

The vigil held for Kurt Cobain at the Seattle
Center International Fountain

Kurt Cobain's house at 171 Lake
Washington Boulevard East

people gathered around the Seattle Center International Fountain for a mass vigil, during which Courtney Love, Cobain's widow, publicly read the suicide note left by her husband.

The impact of grunge is still tangible today, musically, socially, and politically. It was in Seattle, in fact, that the no-global movement took off in 1999, after violent clashes during demonstrations in opposition to the World Trade Organization conference. Just as grunge had opposed luxury and fashion, offering an alternative lifestyle, no-globals pointed a finger at multinational corporations like Microsoft and Starbucks—both from Seattle—and proposed a no-logo, local market economic system.

In the new millennium, Seattle's musical and cultural vitality has not faded, and it continues to be a cradle of new trends, with bands reviving its sounds around the world, such as Death Cab for Cutie, Fleet Foxes, and Car Seat Headrest.

1947 A seventeen-year-old Ray Charles arrives in Seattle and meets Quincy Jones.

1979 Bruce Pavitt launches *Subterranean Pop*.

1962 Elvis Presley films *It Happened at the World's Fair* at Century 21 Exposition, the 1962 World's Fair.

1984 *The Fabulous Sounds of the Pacific Northwest*, the debut album by the Young Fresh Fellows, was given a positive review by *Rolling Stone*.

1963 Jerden Records releases Kingsmen's *Louie Louie*, a controversial track, and it becomes a worldwide hit.

1986 Bruce Pavitt and Jonathan Poneman found Sub Pop Records.

1968 Jimi Hendrix headlines for the first time at Seattle Center Arena.

Some members
of Soundgarden and the future
Pearl Jam release their first
and only record as
Temple of the Dog.

1990

Kurt Cobain dies. **1994**

David Bazan forms
Pedro the Lion. **1995**

The Riot Grrrl feminist movement
is founded in Olympia. **1991**

Clashes during the
World Trade Organization (WTO)
conference bring attention to the
"people of Seattle," one of the
most active and important
no-global movements. **1999**

Nevermind by Nirvana reaches first place in
the rankings.

Cameron Crowe directs *Singles*, a romantic
comedy set in grunge-era Seattle that also
features members of Pearl Jam,
Alice in Chains, and Soundgarden.

1992

Robin Pecknold and Skyler
Skjelset form Fleet Foxes,
one of the most important
groups in contemporary
folk rock revival.

2006

Map of Seattle

1 The Crocodile Cafe
2200 2nd Avenue (original location);
2505 1st Avenue (current location).

2 KEXP 90.3 FM & 91.7 FM
113 Dexter Avenue North (original
location); 472 1st Avenue North (current
location).

3 Black Dog Forge
2316 2nd Avenue.

4 The Vogue
2018 1st Avenue (no longer in existence).
In 1988, it hosted the first Seattle concert
of Nirvana, who opened for Blood Circus
that night.

5 Sub Pop Records
1932 1st Avenue (original location);
2013 4th Avenue (current location).

6 The Showbox
1426 1st Avenue.
Since its cabaret origins in 1939, countless
artists have performed at this club, from
jazz icon Duke Ellington to burlesque queen
Gypsy Rose Lee.

7 Coryell Apartments
1820 East Thomas Street.
The apartment building in which the
protagonists of the film *Singles* live.

8 The Black Elks Club
662½ South Jackson Street, top floor (no
longer in existence).

9 The Black and Tan Club
404½ 12th Avenue South (no longer in
existence).

10 The Blue Moon and Rainbow Taverns
712 & 722 NE 45th Street.
The epicenter of the Seattle beatnik
community, these two taverns are rich
in literary and musical history.

11 Roosevelt High School
1410 NE 66th Street.
Its alumni include Pearl Jam guitarist
Mike McCready, Guns N' Roses bassist
Duff McKagan, and Mötley Crüe bassist
Nikki Sixx.

12 The Moore
1932 2nd Avenue.

13 The 5th Avenue Theatre
1308 5th Avenue.

14 The Paramount
911 Pine Street.

15 Seattle Center International Fountain
305 Harrison Street.

*On pages 16–17
Nirvana plays at the MTV Live and Loud in 1993*

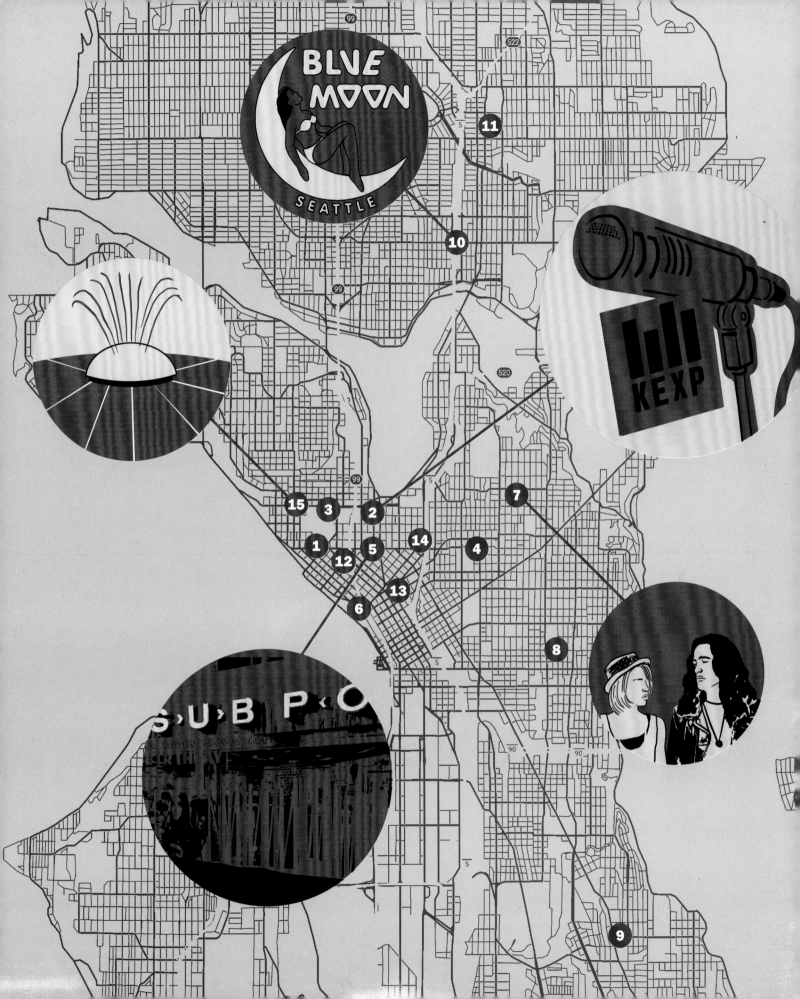

New York City

The early twentieth century was a time of transition for US music, and New York City, for the first of many times in history, would position itself as a hotbed of this transformation.

During the nineteenth century, the most popular genre in the city was Italian opera, which had not only surpassed British opera—imported by the British starting in the mid-eighteenth century—in popularity, but had also contributed to the establishment of several conservatories and two of New York's most important theaters, the Metropolitan Opera (1882) and Carnegie Hall (1891). At the beginning of the new century, however, there was a shift from classical music to more modern styles, such as jazz and blues, and the key figure in the change was George Gershwin. From the moment he was eighteen, he began to write music in Tin Pan Alley, being the first to combine a taste for classical melody with arrangements of new Black sounds. Meanwhile, theaters on Broadway revolutionized the performing arts with the first musicals.

In 1885, many music publishers began opening their agencies on West 28th Street in Manhattan's Flower District. The area was soon nicknamed Tin Pan Alley. With stricter copyright protection laws enacted at the turn of the century, songwriters, composers, lyricists and publishers began to work together to support each other, and Willis Woodard and T.B. Harms were the first publishers to specialize in pop music instead of classical music or hymnals.

Aspiring songwriters, including the famous Irving Berlin, knocked on every agency's door hoping to sell their songs, while "song pluggers," pianists and singers who represented music publishers, made a living playing songs to promote sheet music sales. Among them were George Gershwin, Harry Warren, and Al Sherman.

The 1920s brought another cultural revolution, the Harlem Renaissance, which led to the spread of African American music and art throughout the United States, jazz and blues being the main genres. New York blues, greatly influenced by jazz, displayed a more sophisticated sound than Southern blues. From urban jazz, a new, faster, more rhythmic genre arose: bebop, made famous by musicians such as Dizzy Gillespie, Charlie Parker, and Thelonious Monk. Big bands soon shifted from jazz to swing, a genre that would dominate the music scene for the next two decades.

Beginning in the 1950s, New York City was the center of another movement, the folk music revival, after many young people became interested in Appalachian folk music, blues, and roots styles. Greenwich Village, a young neighborhood with a strong countercultural thrust, became the hotbed of this interest, and one of the first artists to perform in the area's clubs was Joan Baez. A few years later, she introduced a very young Bob Dylan to the public during one of her concerts; he played a key role in the contamination of folk and rock when, in 1965, he released his masterpiece *Like a Rolling Stone*, which ushered in songwriting as we know it today. Bands and songwriters took their cues for songs from their own lives, from literature, and from the world around them—New York—and generated an underground movement that would find its zenith in 1967 in the album *The Velvet Underground & Nico* by the band

of the same name, following the meeting of Lou Reed, John Cale, and Andy Warhol.

In the 1960s, another union created unprecedented music: from the mix of Cuban and Puerto Rican rhythms of

Joan Baez and Bob Dylan in New York during the *Rolling Thunder Revue*, 1975

Hispanic neighborhoods came salsa, a new genre that spread to the city's vibrant big band jazz scene. The huge wave of Puerto Ricans who moved to New York City seeking a new identity in their adopted city began to be reflected in these new, fresh, and rhythmic sounds, which spread from the streets of Spanish Harlem to the rest of the world.

The 1970s brought other new revolutions to New York City. First, disco music. Thousands of young people poured into clubs every night to get lost in the low lights and high bpms, in venues that became iconic, like the legendary Studio 54.

Thanks in part to a blackout that turned the city dark on the night of July 13, 1977, the groundwork was laid for the birth of another fundamental genre: hip-hop. The forced darkness unleashed a wave of violence and raids. Instrument stores were stormed by all those young people who did not have the financial means to buy the basic tools necessary to play and express themselves. New York's DJs and MCs were born that night.

Hip-hop comes, in fact, from block parties, where DJs such as Kool Herc, Grandmaster Flash, and Afrika Bambaataa began isolating beats from funk and R&B pieces, rapping while the audience danced.

New York City was also home to the first documented punk rock scene. Drawing on influences from local artists such as The Velvet Underground and the New York Dolls, punk music developed in CBGB's and Max's Kansas City clubs. Patti Smith, Talking Heads, Blondie, Suicide, Television, and other new wave artists populated the city's music, while the Ramones began experimenting with the sounds that would characterize the new punk rock and the sound of bands such as Swans and Sonic Youth.

With the new millennium, the contemporary scene shifted to Brooklyn, where the bands Yeah Yeah Yeahs, LCD Soundsystem, Animal Collective, and Moldy Peaches flourished, while a frenzy for Julian Casablancas's The Strokes raged in Manhattan amid indie labels, internet radio, and webzines.

⟩ **The legendary entrance of CBGB**

1750

The most famous of ballad operas debuts in New York: *The Beggar's Opera*.

1965

With *Like a Rolling Stone*, Bob Dylan enshrines the fusion of folk and rock.

1882

The Metropolitan Opera House opens.

1967

The Velvet Underground & Nico is released.

1885

A group of music publishers unite to set up shop in the Flower District, launching Tin Pan Alley's fortunes.

1969

A raid on the Stonewall Inn in Greenwich Village kicks off the Stonewall Uprising, in which the homosexual community clashes with the police. The civil rights movement is born, and June 28 is dedicated to LGBTQIA+ pride.

1891

Carnegie Hall is inaugurated.

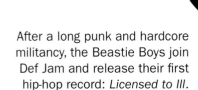

On December 10, CBGB, the world's most iconic rock club, opens in the Bowery.

1973

After a long punk and hardcore militancy, the Beastie Boys join Def Jam and release their first hip-hop record: *Licensed to Ill*.

1986

Studio 54, international temple of disco music, opens on April 26.

At 9:30 p.m. on July 13, the entire city finds itself without power due to a malfunction at a power plant caused by lightning.

1977

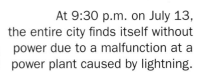

In Staten Island, RZA, GZA, Method Man, and others found Wu-Tang Clan.

1992

A ruthless rivalry between East and West Coast rappers leads to the murder of Notorious B.I.G.

1997

With the collection *No New York*, Brian Eno formalizes the No Wave scene.

1978

With *The Adventures of Grandmaster Flash on the Wheels of Steel*, a DJ releases his own mixtape for the first time.

1981

The Strokes' *Is This It* is released, the album that brings indie rock to the center of the world.

2001

Map of New York City

1 **Studio 54**
254 West 54th Street.

2 **CBGB**
315 Bowery (no longer in existence).

3 **Tin Pan Alley**
West 28th Street, between 5th and 6th
Avenue (no longer in existence).

4 **Birdland**
1678 Broadway (original location);
315 West 44th Street (current location).
The main point of reference for the jazz
community in New York City.

5 **Radio City Music Hall**
1260 6th Avenue.
The New York temple of live music, founded
in 1932.

6 **Apollo Theater**
253 West 125th Street.
The most famous club for African American
musicians in the US, in the heart of Harlem.

7 **Cafe Wha?**
115 MacDougal Street.
The club that hosted Bob Dylan's first
concert and where Jimi Hendrix decided to
leave for London with The Animals.

8 **Jones Street & West 4th Street**
Location of the photo of Bob Dylan and
Suze Rotolo that ended up on the cover of
The Freewheelin' Bob Dylan.

9 **Chelsea Hotel**
222 West 23rd Street.
Smith, Leonard Cohen, and Janis Joplin
passed through the rooms of the Chelsea
Hotel before it made headlines for the death
of Nancy Spungen, girlfriend of Sid Vicious.

10 **The Dakota**
1 West 72nd Street.
The Dakota has been home to many artists,
including John Lennon, who was murdered
outside the building in 1980.

11 **Strawberry Fields**
Central Park West at West 72nd Street.
A John Lennon memorial in the heart
of Central Park.

12 **Carnegie Hall**
881 7th Avenue.

13 **Joe Strummer Memorial**
132 East 7th Street.
Made in 2003 by Dr. Revolt to commemorate
Strummer, a regular at nearby bar Niagara.

14 **The Music Inn**
169 West 4th Street.
Opened in 1958, the Music Inn is one of the
city's most historic music stores.

15 **The Bitter End**
147 Bleecker Street.
Dubbed "the oldest rock and roll club in New
York City," its founding dates back to 1961.

16 **Trash and Vaudeville**
96 East 7th Street.
Punk boutique that opened in 1975 and point
of reference for The Clash.

17 **Electric Lady Studios**
52 West 8th Street.
In search of a cheap, self-contained recording
venue, Jimi Hendrix purchased the building in
1968 to turn it into a studio.

18 **Brill Building**
1619 Broadway.
In 1962, 165 music publishers were based here.

Los Angeles

Los Angeles has had an unparalleled contribution to music history. Not only has it always served as fertile ground for the discovery of global phenomena, but it is also home to some of the world's leading music studios and labels. And the presence of Hollywood and its film industry has acted and continues to act as a driving force for new sources of inspiration for music in the "Golden City."

Founded by a Spanish governor in 1781, capital of the Mexican region of Alta California and conquered in 1847 by the United States, Los Angeles has always been a crossroads of cultures, and so has its music.

The 1920s and '30s saw African American music flourish in the city, and jazz became the most popular genre, with a sound characterized by unconventional rhythms, rapid key changes, and quirky melodies. Jazz musicians' favorite instruments were the drums, piano, and saxophone, and improvisation played a key role in which artists used to invent their own tunes directly on stage.

Ritchie Valens

The heart of jazz was Central Avenue: in the clubs that dotted the neighborhood, Charles Mingus, Buddy Collette, and Charlie Parker left indelible marks on the city's sounds with their performances. Today this legacy has been picked up by musicians such as Thundercat and Kamasi Washington, who have cast a wider genre net by grafting other typically Los Angeles experiences onto it, that of rap.

The influence of Latin culture brought by Mexican immigrants has also always been particularly relevant in the city. With the infusion of the fast rhythms of mariachi music into the increasingly popular rock and roll, Los Angeles in the 1950s saw the rise of Chicano rock. East Los Angeles was the epicenter.

One of the pioneers of the genre was Ritchie Valens, author of the famous song "La Bamba." Despite his untimely death in 1959 due to a plane crash that also claimed the lives of two other music legends, Buddy Holly and The Big Bopper, on the day known as "the day that music died," his music paved the way for future icons of the genre, such as Los Lobos and War.

From folk to psychedelia, more sophisticated experimentation to the pure energy of electric guitars, the 1960s were swept up in the wave of rock music. In 1961, three brothers began jamming with their cousin, writing songs with simple melodies, harmonized vocals, and lyrics centered around surf life. Soon a schoolmate joined them as well. Their first concert was actually at the Ritchie Valens Memorial Dance, and the highlight of the performance was "Surfin' Safari." They were The Beach Boys, and that night, for the first of many times in their careers, they revolutionized the course of music history.

At the same time, far from the beaches and sheltered in the Hollywood Hills, Laurel Canyon became the birthplace of a counterculture. The neighborhood was home to Cass Elliot of the Mamas & the Papas, Joni Mitchell, Frank Zappa, Jim Morrison of The Doors, Carole King, The Byrds, Buffalo Springfield, Love, Neil Young, Brian Wilson of The Beach Boys, James Taylor, and Jackson Browne. The home of "Mama" Cass Elliot was host to wild parties that became the inspiration for the song "Twelve Thirty (Young Girls Are Coming to the Canyon)," released by the group in 1967. Joni Mitchell dedicated her third album, 1970's *Ladies of the Canyon*, to life in the neighborhood community, and the house she lived in is the one sung in the same year by Crosby, Stills, and Nash in "Our House," written by her then-lover, Graham Nash.

The Beach Boys on stage at Whisky a Go Go in 1970

This creative buzz continued into the 1970s when bands like The Doors continued to reign over Sunset Strip with their fiery performances at Whisky a Go Go.

Los Angeles nights were also beginning to glow with a different light, that of Black music, which was moving from the Midwest to the West Coast.

Motown, the Detroit-based label that had contributed to the birth and spread of soul and R&B in the 1960s, moved its offices to Sunset Boulevard, and Earth, Wind & Fire, Marvin Gaye, and Stevie Wonder came to town, sparking a veritable Black Renaissance.

The 1980s brought a new genre to the forefront that came not from the inner cities but from a southern suburb of the city: Compton. It was there that gangsta rap was born. The center of this was the Eve's After Dark nightclub, which had a recording studio and became the musical laboratory for many artists, including the father of California gangsta rap, Dr. Dre, and World Class Wreckin' Cru. One night in 1987, while they were in the studio with a stack of rhymes written by O'Shea "Ice Cube" Jackson, Andre "Dr. Dre" Young urged Eric "Eazy-E" Wright to take the microphone and begin rapping the lyrics to a song describing the everyday life of a Compton gangster, "Boyz-N-the-Hood." Hip-hop changed forever. Their group, N.W.A, inspired entire generations of

Los Angeles artists, such as Tupac Shakur, Snoop Dogg, Coolio, and Kendrick Lamar.

The 1980s also saw the rise of another movement formed by bands that incorporated psychedelia, rich vocal harmonies, and guitar riffs and stood as direct descendants of the bands of the 1960s, giving rise to a rock revival: Paisley Underground. Its leading exponents, The Dream Syndicate, attracted attention for their feedback-soaked instrumental improvisations, an impetus for the evolution of underground rock in the city that came with Opal, later known as Mazzy Star.

At the same time, the hard rock movement was taking hold, thanks to one of the world's most famous rock bands, Guns N' Roses. Meanwhile, rock was drawing influences from other genres with the rise of bands like Tool and Red Hot Chili Peppers.

Even today, the City of Stars continues to retain its importance as the center of the American pop music industry, giving rise to constellations of artists and phenomena destined to leave a mark on the world's musical imagination.

Flea of the Red Hot Chili Peppers in concert in Los Angeles

1919 The Los Angeles Philharmonic gives their first performance.

1966 The Beatles play at Dodger Stadium on August 28. It is the penultimate concert of their career.

Los Angeles' first radio station opens.

1922

The Hollywood Bowl opens.

1970 Janis Joplin is found lifeless from an overdose in room 105 of the Landmark Hotel.

1940 Hollywood Palladium opens with a concert by Frank Sinatra and the Tommy Dorsey Orchestra.

1985 Guns N' Roses make their debut at the Troubadour on June 6.

A ruthless rivalry between East and West Coast rappers leads to the September 7 injury and murder of Tupac Shakur.

1996

N.W.A releases *Straight Outta Compton*.

1988

Britney Spears shoots the video for "Baby One More Time" at Venice High School.

1998

River Phoenix dies of a drug overdose outside the Viper Room, the club owned by friend Johnny Depp.

1993

Rage Against the Machine plays outside the Staples Center during the Democratic National Convention. The riot that breaks out at the end of the show leads to several arrests.

2000

Map of Los Angeles

1 United Western Recorders
6000/6050 Sunset Boulevard (no longer in existence).
It was here that Frank Sinatra recorded his records for *Reprise* and that Brian Wilson gave birth to such masterpieces as *Pet Sounds* and *Smile* by the Beach Boys.

2 Capitol Records Tower
1750 Vine Street.
Designed and built to resemble a record tower, Nat King Cole built his fortune between its circular walls.

3 Whisky a Go Go
8901 Sunset Boulevard.

4 Viper Room
8852 Sunset Boulevard.

5 The Troubador
9081 Santa Monica Boulevard.
It was an important center for folk music in the 1960s and later for rock.

6 Rainbow Bar and Grill
9015 Sunset Boulevard.
From Elvis Presley to Keith Moon, Alice Cooper to Ringo Starr, the Hollywood Vampires to the Red Hot Chili Peppers, the venue has been, and still is, one of the music scene's main gathering places.

7 Amoeba Music
6200 Hollywood Boulevard.
There is no record collector who does not dream of setting foot in there at least once.

8 Canter's
419 North Fairfax Avenue.
A Jewish deli that became the hot spot of the glam rock and hair rock scene in the 1980s.

9 Chateau Marmont
8221 Sunset Boulevard.
Its cottages have hosted the most famous names in showbiz.

10 Highland Garden Hotel
7047 Franklin Avenue.
When it was still the Landmark Hotel, it was the den of alternative and bohemian artists, including Jimi Hendrix, Jim Morrison, and Alice Cooper.

11 Hollywood Bowl
2301 North Highland Avenue.
One of the best concert arenas in the US.

12 Walt Disney Concert Hall
111 South Grand Avenue.
Designed by Frank O. Gehry, it is the home of the Los Angeles Philharmonic Orchestra.

13 Eve's After Dark
12823 South Avalon Boulevard (no longer in existence).

14 Fivestar Studios
Topanga Canyon.
One of the last recording studios in operation with all-analog instrumentation, it is owned by singer-songwriter Jonathan Wilson.

15 Elliott Smith Memorial "Figure 8"
4334 West Sunset Boulevard.
The mural Elliott Smith leaned on in the iconic *Figure 8* cover is now a memorial in memory of the singer-songwriter.

On pages 40–41
Walt Disney Concert Hall

San Francisco

"If you're going to San Francisco, be sure to wear some flowers in your hair." This verse from the most famous song by Scott McKenzie, "San Francisco (Be Sure to Wear Some Flowers in Your Hair)," released in 1967 and immediately the ballad of the "Summer of Love," which had infected the Californian city that year.

The San Francisco music scene is one of the most famous in the United States and has given birth to such diverse and influential experiences as Journey, the Grateful Dead, Jefferson Airplane, Janis Joplin, Dave Brubeck, Sylvester, Boz Scaggs, the Steve Miller Band, and Etta James.

The true epicenter of the revolutions of the 1960s was the Haight-Ashbury district. The term "Summer of Love" comes from the gathering of nearly 100,000 hippies that took place during the summer of 1967 in the very neighborhood that became the center of youth counterculture, creative expression, drugs, and freedom. The "Summer of Love" contributed to the spread of a new musical genre, acid rock, and the debut of the Grateful Dead and

Aretha Franklin and Ray Charles in concert at the Fillmore, San Francisco

Janis Joplin, artists who symbolized an entire generation.

The Fillmore, on the other hand, is a district full of theaters, dance halls, nightclubs, and clubs whose history and influence dates back to the early 1930s. Jack's Tavern opened in 1933, shortly followed by the Club Alabam and the Town Club, venues that ignited the city's jazz scene and ushered in a new era of African American music, which made Fillmore "the Harlem of the West." Famed promoter Bill Graham, before running the historic theater that bears the district's name, began his career organizing concerts in a neighborhood dance hall in 1965. The Fillmore Theatre became the heart of psychedelic rock and counterculture, hosting bands such as the Grateful Dead, the Steve Miller Band, Santana, The Who, The Doors, and The Jimi Hendrix Experience on its stage. In those years, the venue also became famous for its posters, with which it advertised psychedelic music events that radically changed the world of graphic design and visual communication. The concert posters, as psychedelic as the music, had flamboyant, rounded lettering like bubbles and colors that resembled those of the lava lamps that stood in the rooms of all flower children. The protagonist of this evolution was a local artist named Wes Wilson, whose concert designs for Santana, Muddy Waters, and even The Beatles, full of color in stark contrast to the black-and-white beatnik iconography, became the signature style of the American counterculture.

But the Fillmore's doors were not only open to the roaring guitars of the psychedelic generation. Miles Davis, Aretha Franklin, and Otis Redding performed there, and it remains a hot spot in the city's music scene to this day.

The Matrix, on the other hand, was the first venue to host folk music, helping to shape the San Francisco Sound. It opened on August 13, 1965, presenting Jefferson Airplane, which singer Marty Balin had created to be the club's resident band. The group quickly rose to prominence with its performances at the Matrix thanks in part to noted music critic Ralph J. Gleason, who, after witnessing one of their performances at the club, became one of their early supporters and promoters. The Matrix was also the favorite hangout of Hunter S. Thompson, inventor of gonzo journalism and editor and contributor to *Rolling Stone* magazine, founded in 1967 in San Francisco, and he included the Matrix in his most iconic book, *Fear and Loathing in Las Vegas*.

North Beach, on the other hand, is the home of jazz. In the 1950s, it was the city's

Flyer made by Wes Wilson for a concert by the Grateful Dead

Green Day performing in San Francisco

bohemian neighborhood, chosen as the place of choice by members of the Beat Generation. Jack Kerouac, Neal Cassady, Gary Snyder, and Michael McClure would spend time sipping coffee and listening to the heartfelt sounds of jazz at the Jazz Workshop, where Miles Davis, Cannonball Adderley, Gerry Mulligan, Stan Getz, Horace Silver, John Coltrane, and Dizzy Gillespie performed. The neighborhood is also credited with the beginnings of stand-up comedy, with comedians such as Lenny Bruce, Mort Sahl, and Dick Gregory; poetry readings accompanied by the jazz of Lawrence Ferlinghetti, an iconic figure in the city's history; coffeehouses; folk clubs; and strip clubs. The counterculture revolution that took place in the city in the 1960s could not have taken place without the Beat Generation paving the way in the previous decade with its cultural values, such as spiritual quests, exploration of Western and Eastern religions, experimentation with psychedelic drugs, rejection of materialism, and sexual freedom and exploration.

The free love and peace anthems of the 1960s were, however, followed by the restlessness of the next generation, and in the late 1970s, San Francisco saw the emergence of punk music. Like the earlier city cultural experiences, punk was characterized by a strong antiestablishment spirit, opposing the political status quo with grit and fierce criticism. Pioneering the genre in the city were the Dead Kennedys. On January 14, 1978, the Sex Pistols held their last concert at San Francisco's Winterland Ballroom: the show was opened by the Nuns and the Avengers, two local punk bands who let the world know that night that the city had its own thriving scene ready to explode.

The influence of the British post-punk bands that dominated the European music scenes in the late 1970s and 1980s came to the American rock scene in the late 1990s and helped to revive punk with new sounds, such as those of Green Day and Rancid. But the American 1980s and 1990s were also the decades of pure rock, to which San Francisco contributed with bands like Counting Crows, Third Eye Blind, and Metallica, who settled there in those years.

Today, San Francisco continues to be a center of innovation and experimentation, with musicians constantly seeking new sounds and innovative styles: Devendra Banhart, Ben Chasny and the Six Organs of Admittance, and the Brian Jonestown Massacre are just some of the names bringing the city's new sound to the world.

On pages 48–49
Two legs stick out the window of the Piedmont Boutique in the Haight-Ashbury district

1922

The Castro Theatre is inaugurated, which will become a hub for the LGBTQIA+ community.

1967

The year of the "Summer of Love." More than 100,000 people gather in the Haight-Ashbury neighborhood to celebrate peace and free love.

Rolling Stone is founded.

1953

Lawrence Ferlinghetti and Peter D. Martin found the independent bookstore and publishing house City Lights, which first publishes Allen Ginsberg's controversial poem *Howl*.

1968

St. John Coltrane African Orthodox Church is founded, the only house of worship in the United States dedicated to the message and music of John Coltrane.

1965   The Matrix opens.

The Sex Pistols hold their last concert at Winterland Ballroom.

On August 13, 25,000 people gather at Polo Fields in Golden Gate Park to honor Jerry Garcia, the voice and guitarist of the Grateful Dead, who died four days earlier.

1995

Harvey Milk is elected to city council. He is the first elected representative from a major US city to be openly gay.

1978

Devendra Banhart leaves San Francisco Art Institute to focus on his career as a singer-songwriter.

2000

With *Dookie*, Green Day sells more than twenty million copies.

1994

E-40, Mistah F.A.B., Too $hort, and Keak Da Sneak bring to prominence the Hyphy Movement, one of the largest hip-hop scenes in the US.

2006

Map of San Francisco

1   The Fillmore
1805 Geary Boulevard.

2   The Matrix
3138 Fillmore Street.

3   Great American Music Hall
859 O'Farrell Street.

4   The Chapel
777 Valencia Street.

5   Amoeba Music
1855 Haight Street.

6   Candlestick Park
602 Jamestown Avenue.
It hosted the last date of The Beatles' final
tour on August 29, 1966.

7   Grateful Dead House
710 Ashbury Street.

8   Jimi Hendrix House
1524A Haight Street.

9   Janis Joplin House
635 Ashbury Street.

10   Sly and the Family Stone House
700 Urbana Street.
After his first hit, nineteen-year-old Sly
Stone buys his parents this house in
Ingleside, keeping the basement apartment
for himself. It is here that Sly and the
Family Stone are formed.

11   SFJAZZ Center
201 Franklin Street.
Concert space for jazz artists and museum
on the history of the genre. Each year it
hosts the San Francisco Jazz Festival, one
of the world's premier jazz showcases.

12   Rod's Hickory Pit
199 Lincoln Road West, Vallejo.
Although just outside of town, this historic
diner hosted some of Green Day's
earliest performances.

13   City Lights Bookstore
261-271 Columbus Avenue.
The independent bookstore founded
at the Lawrence Ferlinghetti and Peter
D. Martin hangout of the Beat Generation.

The window of City Lights Bookstore

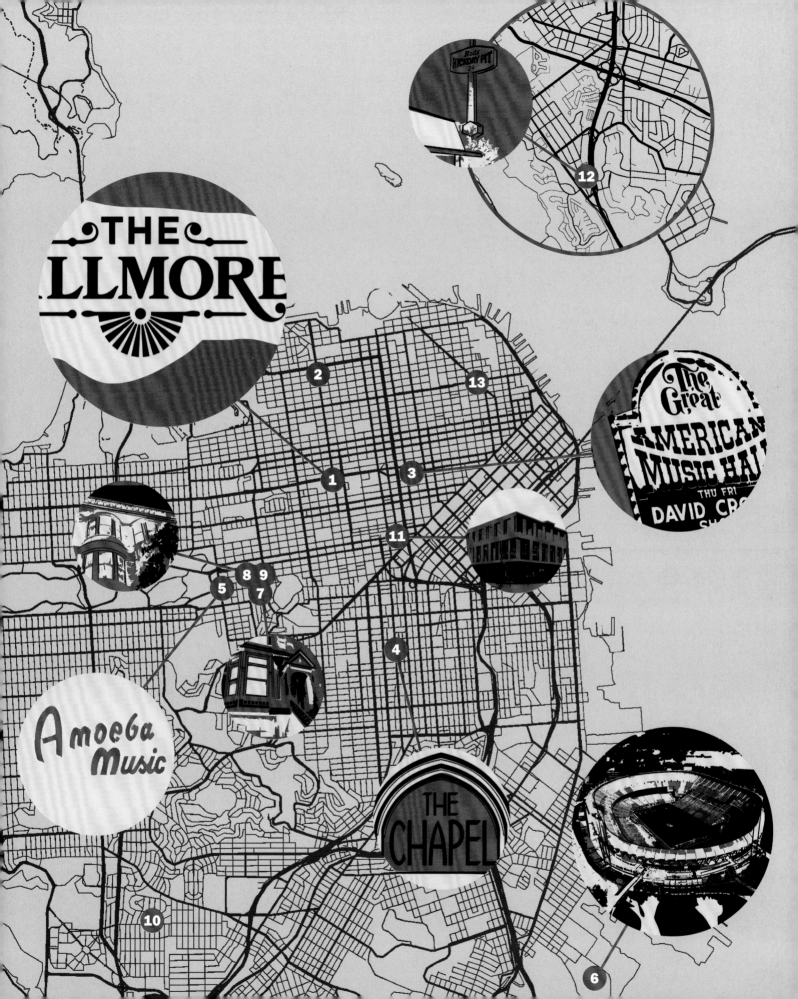

THE FILLMORE

THE Great AMERICAN MUSIC HALL
THU FRI
DAVID CRO

Amoeba Music

THE CHAPEL

Nashville

Of all the cities in the world that can boast a close tie to music, only one can officially call itself "Music City": Nashville.

Music history in the capital of Tennessee began back in 1700 when the first French settlers celebrated their arrival on the banks of the Cumberland River with the playing of violins and long traditional balls. The first "celebrity" from Nashville was Davy Crockett, a famous frontiersman and member of Congress, known all over not only for his heroic stories but also for his skill on the violin.

In the second half of the nineteenth century, the Fisk Jubilee Singers, an African American a cappella group from Fisk University, were the first artists in history to do a world tour. After the civil war, their concerts not only helped finance the education and college admission of African Americans who were previously slaves but also put Nashville on the map as a global hub of music. Legend has it that when they played for Queen Victoria of England, she said the band must come from a "city of music," coining the term still used today to refer to Nashville.

The neon signs of honky-tonks on Lower Broadway, Nashville

Ryman Auditorium, home of the Grand Ole Opry

radio program the Grand Ole Opry, presenting fiddler Uncle Jimmy Thompson as the first performer of a new show that was first called "The WSM Barn Dance." The number of listeners grew quickly thanks to the choice of guests and broadcasting on Saturday. It ended up getting picked up by NBC in 1939. Since then, the Opry has launched the careers of many country music singers, including Loretta Lynn, Dolly Parton, and Bill Anderson.

In 1974, the Grand Ole Opry moved from Ryman Auditorium to its new home in the Opry House, where it still exists today. The show is still broadcast weekly, almost one hundred years since its start, making it the longest-running radio program in America and helping to legitimize Nashville as Music City. According to another tale, it was WSM announcer David Cobb who gave the city its nickname during the program in 1950.

At the end of the century, Ryman Auditorium, inaugurated in 1892, became one of the most famous halls in the country thanks to its location, which was central back then, and its excellent natural acoustics. In 1925, Nashville further consolidated its national fame when the city radio station WSM (whose signal reached the entire US) chose Ryman as the home for the

In the 1930s, not far from Fisk University, Jefferson Street quickly became a center of entertainment, music, and nightlife. On the famous street, a stage for Nashville's rhythm and blues, you could find speakeasies, supper clubs, dance halls, and clubs. In the 1960s, Billy Cox and Jimi Hendrix had a residency at Club Del Morocco, while artists like Otis Redding, Little Richard, Etta James, and many others played at the clubs on the street, transforming it into the cradle of R&B music.

In 1942, the king of country music Roy Acuff and singer Fred Rose founded Acuff-Rose, the first music publishing house in Nashville. Acuff-Rose published hundreds of historical songs, including "I'm So Lonesome I Could Cry" by Hank Williams, "Oh, Pretty Woman" by Roy Orbison, and "Bye Bye Love" by the Everly Brothers.

In 1954, brothers Owen and Harold Bradley bought a house at 804 16th Avenue South, in the area now known as Music Row, and transformed it into a recording studio, Quonset Hut Studio. Artists like Bob Dylan, Elvis Costello, Lynn Anderson, Ray Price, Johnny Cash, and June Carter Cash, among others, have passed through their halls. Today "the Row" is the center of the music industry in Nashville, the beating heart of Music City.

In 1966, Bob Dylan decided to move to Nashville to record. He made three albums there, *Blonde on Blonde*, *John Wesley Harding*, and *Nashville Skyline*. Due to his presence, Joan Baez, The Byrds, Neil Young, and many others soon arrived in Tennessee.

Still today, the name of Nashville is closely

Johnny Cash

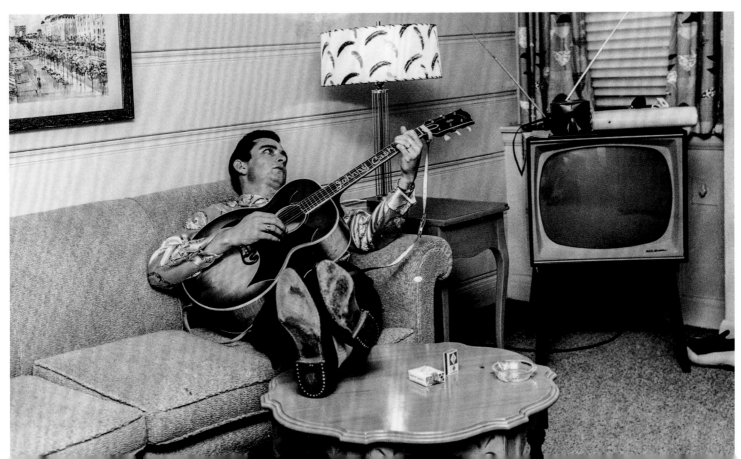

tied to country music. Like many forms of popular music, country has changed over time. It started to develop in the 1920s as a mix of "hillbilly" sounds from Appalachian folk music, Western swing music, and even blues. It shifted to bluegrass and honky-tonk in the 1940s before becoming the more sophisticated "sound of Nashville" of the 1950s and '60s. "Nashville Sound," conceived as a way to boost country sales, which had been devastated by the rise of rock and roll, was known for its smooth strings and choruses, polished voices and soft rhythms, closer to traditional pop music.

Country music has always been rooted in Tennessee (that's where it is believed to have originated, particularly from Bristol in the 1920s), and today "Nashville Sound" continues to triumph across the entire US on radio and Billboard charts.

But over time, Music City has become a home for all music genres, and many global stars have started their careers right in Nashville: Sheryl Crow, Black Eyed Peas, Bon Jovi, Michael Bublé, Kid Rock, Kings of Leon, and The White Stripes. Singer and guitarist Jack White opened an office of his visionary label Third Man Records there in 2009. It has a record store, offices, the label's distribution center, photo studio, and the Third Man Record Booth, the only live studio in the world that can record directly on vinyl.

Nashville is also home to United Record Pressing, the largest vinyl record plant in North America. Opened in 1949, it has printed vinyl for major artists from Miles Davis and Bob Dylan to The Beatles, Beyoncé, Justin Timberlake, and Ludacris.

And the city's music scene continues to grow. In a city full of musicians, you never know who will show up: country music star Blake Shelton, for example, is known for stopping by unannounced at his restaurant Ole Red and playing a few songs. The history of music is written every day in Music City, thanks to the artists who got their starts there or chose to spend time there to write their songs, from Taylor Swift, Bully, and Soccer Mommy to Kesha and the Cyrus family.

Nashville headquarters of Third Man Records

1871 The Fisk Jubilee Singers begin their career.

1954 Quonset Hut Studio, the first recording studio in town, opens.

1892 Ryman Auditorium is inaugurated.

1925 On November 28, WSM radio station begins the "Grand Ole Opry" broadcast with a performance from Uncle Jimmy Thompson.

1961 The Country Music Association establishes the Country Music Hall of Fame, which over the years will expand first with the Country Music Foundation and then with the museum.

1942 Acuff-Rose is Nashville's first music publishing house.

The Opry House opens, which still hosts the Grand Ole Opry broadcast and numerous live shows today. **1974**

From New York, Bob Dylan travels to Nashville to record *Blonde on Blonde* at Nashville's Columbia Recording Studios. **1966**

Garth Brooks releases his eponymous debut album and becomes the world's best-selling solo artist. His success sparks the country music boom in the 1990s. **1989**

Bob Dylan and Johnny Cash meet in Nashville to work together on some tracks for *Nashville Skyline*, the album Dylan was recording in the city. **1969**

Jack White opens the Nashville location of Third Man Records. **2009**

Map of Nashville

1 Ryman Auditorium
116 5th Avenue North.
The mecca of country music.

2 The Opry House
600 Opry Mills Drive.

3 The Bluebird Café
4104 Hillsboro Pike.
The club where even the most famous
songwriters take to the stage to share
their stories and play small, intimate,
impromptu sets.

4 Ole Red
300 Broadway.

5 Third Man Records
623 7th Avenue South.

**6 Country Music Hall of Fame
and Museum**
222 Rep. John Lewis Way
South. One of the world's
largest museums
and research centers
dedicated to the
preservation and
study of American folk
music.

7 Hatch Show Print
224 Rep. John Lewis Way South.
Since its opening in 1879, this print
shop, which was opened by the Hatch
brothers, has designed and printed most
of the posters and playbills for shows and
concerts in the city.

8 Music City Walk of Fame
121 4th Avenue South.
Inside the Nashville Music Garden, there is
a long sidewalk dotted with stars dedicated

to musicians who have made their mark
on the music industry.

9 Cannery Ballroom
1 Cannery Row.
A country music hall opened in the
late 1970s, the venue became one of
Nashville's premier music venues of the
1980s and 1990s.

Left: The logo of Country Music Hall of Fame and Museum
Right: The historic sign of the Bluebird Café

MUSIC CITY
WALK OF FAME PARK

The Music City Walk of Fame
on Nashville's Music Mile
is dedicated to honoring the diverse
musical contributions of the many
individuals who have kept the music
playing in Music City and throughout
the world.

A project of the Nashville Convention &
Visitors Bureau Foundation Music City, Inc.
and Metro Parks.

HATCH
SHOW
PRINT
NASHVILLE
TENNESSEE

Memphis

The history of music in Memphis is as old as the city itself. Sitting on the banks of the Mississippi River between three states, Tennessee, Arkansas, and Mississippi, at the beginning of the nineteenth century, Memphis was a major intersection for commerce and African American culture and an important gateway for people and Mississippi Delta culture passing through on their way north. The spiritual traditions passed down from generation to generation of African Americans subjected to slavery became the basis for blues music and a source of inspiration for artists like W.C. Handy. Known also as the "Father of Blues," he and his band reached Memphis in 1909 to play in the clubs of Beale Street. He was one of the first to play the new and unique style of Memphis blues, an evolution of folk music that developed from the songs sung on plantations and in the fields at the beginning of the century. The key elements of the genre include a drawn-out, slow, repetitive, almost trance-like rhythm, call-and-response lyrics, and "blue notes," intentionally off-tune notes used to evoke emotions.

ed their songs in Memphis and performed regularly on Beale Street.

Gospel music was also important to the rise of the music scene in Memphis. It was at East Trigg Baptist Church that Reverend Herbert Brewster began to write his gospel songs in the 1930s, including classics like "Move On Up a Little Higher" recorded by Mahalia Jackson, and "Surely God Is Able" recorded by the Ward Singers.

After Handy, the blues, and World War II, another revolution shook the city in 1945. With the arrival of the electric guitar, the acoustic and intimate sounds of the blues were the root of the electric sparks of rock and roll. The musical tradition of Memphis shaped the first rockabilly style associated with Elvis Presley, Jerry Lee Lewis, Roy Orbison, Carl Perkins, and Johnny Cash. All five artists did their first real recordings under the guidance of producer Sam Phillips, who is considered one of the fathers of rock and roll, at the Sun Records studio located a few blocks from the heart of the African American nightlife district.

In 1950, Sam Phillips started Sun Studio, merging Memphis Recording Service and Sun Records. According to legend, it was

> **Headquarters of Sun Studio at 706 Union Avenue**

W.C. Handy

Beale Street, one of the first African American nightlife neighborhoods in the US, was known as the "Home of the Blues" and is where W.C. Handy wrote "Memphis Blues" in 1912, which would introduce the genre to the entire country on the radio, changing forever the history of music. Blues legends like Furry Lewis, Little Junior Parker, B.B. King, Howlin' Wolf, Walter Horton, and Joe Hill Louis record-

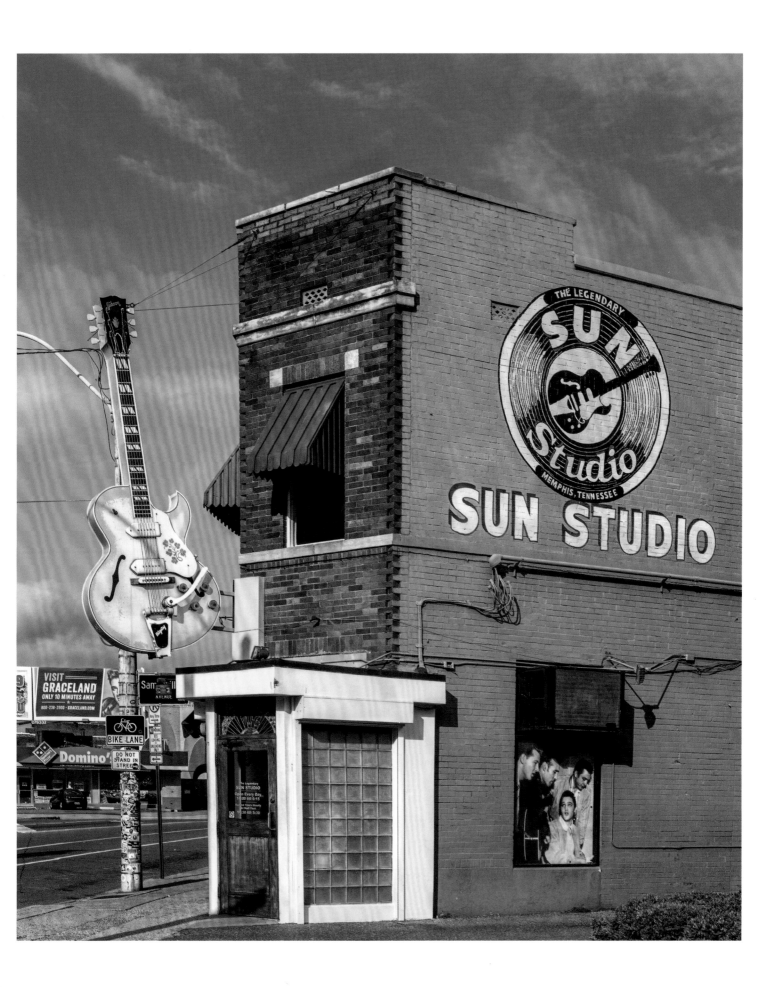

here in April 1951 that the first rock and roll record was made: "Rocket 88" by Jackie Brenston & His Delta Cats, bringing to life the genre, thanks also to the work of artists like B.B. King and Ike Turner, in addition to those already noted. Phillips's time at Sun ended in 1969 with the sale of the label and studios.

Presley, Lewis, Perkins, and Cash managed to show how the rural traditions of the South mixed with the urban rhythms of the city. Although at the time he was living in Memphis, Presley was from northern Mississippi; Perkins was from a rural area of western Tennessee; Lewis came from Louisiana, and Cash from Arkansas. Although Presley went down in history as a rock and roll star, he was very proud of his gospel music recordings, which won Grammy Awards. Lewis, Perkins, and Cash were later identified as country music artists, but despite these attempts to define them, they remained diverse in their music tastes and influences, which meant they couldn't be pigeonholed into one specific genre. At the end of the 1990s, after the deaths of Elvis and Roy Orbison, Lewis's health problems and the decline of Perkins's career following the end of Sun, Johnny Cash was the only one of the five Sun artists to continue recording regularly, and he remained solidly anchored in his unique sound, which was still relevant decades later.

When we speak about the record labels from Memphis that were the first to reach the stars, it's impossible not to mention Satellite Records, founded by Estelle Stewart Axton and her brother Jim Stewart in an abandoned grocery store in Brunswick, in rural Shelby County. In 1960, they moved to an old cinema on 924 East McLemore Avenue in Memphis, where they joined forces with producer Lincoln "Chips" Moman. The first artists to work with Satellite Records included Steve Cropper, Rufus, and Carla Thomas. At the end of 1961, Satellite Records became Stax Records. Booker T. & the M.G.'s were the first stars of the new label. Otis Redding soon joined the roster of the company. Later, Stax Records became an institution of popular American music with artists like Redding, Percy Sledge, and Sam & Dave, especially between 1965 and 1970—a golden period before it was forced to close in 1975—when it put Memphis soul, gospel, funk, and the Delta blues on the map, holding its own against Motown in Detroit. Memphis musician and singer Isaac Hayes wrote many of the label's big successes and became the highest-selling artist with the soundtrack to the film *Shaft* in 1971.

At the beginning of 1969, with his film work ending and the famous *'68 Comeback Special* behind him, Elvis Presley was ready

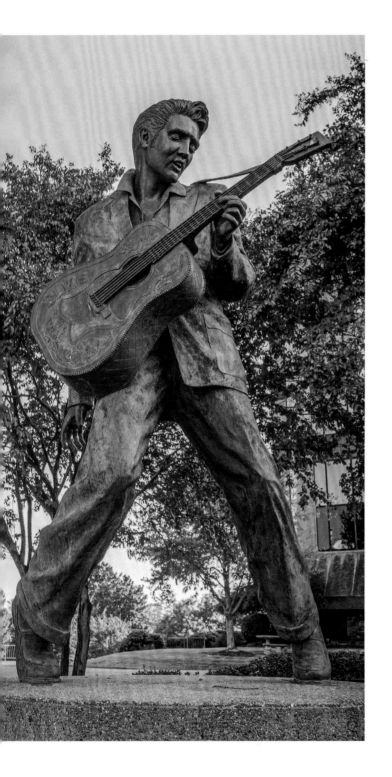

to start seriously recording again. He didn't have to go far to find the hottest band, producer, and studio around. Over the years, Lincoln "Chips" Moman and his American Sound Studio had become a giant, and Moman recruited an exceptional number of musicians from the house bands of Hi Records and Phillips Records to create the "Memphis Boys." With Moman producing, the house band would become a hit machine by the second half of the 1960s, churning out a string of songs topping charts for artists like Box Tops ("The Letter"), Dusty Springfield ("Son of a Preacher Man"), Neil Diamond ("Sweet Caroline"), B.J. Thomas ("Hooked on a Feeling"), and Bobby Womack ("Fly Me to the Moon").

Elvis's sessions in 1969 in Memphis marked the musical rebirth of the King, who that same year returned to performing live full time.

❮ The statue of the King of Rock and Roll in the square named after him, Elvis Presley Plaza

1909

W.C. Handy, the Father of Blues, arrives with his band in Memphis and establishes his home base on Beale Street.

1957

Stax Records, initially called Satellite Records, is founded in Memphis.

1950

Sam Phillips founds Sun Studio.

1968

Martin Luther King Jr. is assassinated on a balcony on the second floor of the Lorraine Motel.

1951

"Rocket 88," considered the first rock and roll 45, is recorded at Sun Studio.

The compilation album *Beale Street Saturday Night* is released. Recorded at Ardent Studios, the record is a sort of audio tour of Memphis at a difficult time for the city, which is in steep decline after the assassination of Martin Luther King Jr.

1979

Elvis Presley joins Chips Moman and the Memphis Boys in the studio.

1969

Three 6 Mafia win an Oscar for Best Original Song for "It's Hard Out Here for a Pimp," from Terence Howard's film *Hustle & Flow*.

2006

Billy Lee Riley, cult rock and roll artist, considered by many to be the lost talent of Sun Records, dies.

2009

Map of Memphis

1 Beale Street
The street where the Delta blues was born. It is still one of the city's main attractions today, thanks to the many clubs and restaurants located along the street where the notes that made Memphis one of America's music capitals continue to play. Some of the clubs that keep the city's nights bustling and the museums that preserve its history are:

2 BB King's Blues Club
143 Beale Street.

3 Jerry Lee Lewis' Cafe & Honky Tonk
310 Beale Street.

4 Rum Boogie Cafe
182 Beale Street.

5 W.C. Handy Memphis Home and Museum
352 Beale Street.
The house museum of the "Father of Blues."

6 Memphis Rock 'n' Soul Museum
191 Beale Street.
Passing through its halls, you can trace the history of the city's music from the pioneers to the present day.

7 Sun Studio
706 Union Avenue.

8 Graceland
3734 Elvis Presley Boulevard.
The legendary home of Elvis Presley.

9 Stax Museum of American Soul Music
926 East McLemore Avenue.
The museum dedicated to the history of the label and the genre it helped make great.

10 Memphis Music Hall of Fame Museum
126 South Second Street.
Established to celebrate and honor great Memphis artists, it opened an exhibition space in 2015 that can be visited.

11 Ardent Studios
2000 Madison Avenue.
Founded by John Fry and initially located in his family's garage, where he recorded his first 45s for the Ardent Records label.

12 The Arcade Restaurant
540 South Main Street.
The oldest diner in Memphis, as well as Elvis's favorite, still retains the look it had in the 1950s.

"I Got Everything I Need" di Sam & Dave, lato B del singolo di successo "Hold On! I'm Coming"

On pages 74–75
Stax Museum of
American Soul Music

Austin

Nashville may have claimed the nickname "Music City," but Austin is known as the "Live Music Capital of the World."

Part of the credit is due to Willie Nelson, the legendary country singer-songwriter. The music scene in Austin developed around First Street and Barton Springs Road, where the Armadillo World Headquarters stands, which is one of the clubs where—legend has it—Willie Nelson united two countercultures that couldn't be more distant and opposing: hippy and redneck. This union sparked the birth of a vibrant music scene that today is called roots music, or better yet, Americana.

The first European colonists—mainly from Germany and Sweden—and Mexicans brought their musical heritage here. Even back in 1870, the city teemed with German breweries. Today, the oldest operating restaurant west of the Mississippi River is the Scholz Garten on San Jacinto Boulevard. Its live music program was able to attract some interesting figures back

B.B. King in concert in Austin

in the day, including General Custer, who was stationed in the cavalry in Texas at the time. The beer garden has a large outdoor stage with the German Alps painted on the background; it remains a must-see spot.

In the 1920s, Austin became the seat of numerous jazz bars, including the famous Victory Grill. In the 1930s and '40s, country music and big bands took over the scene. In 1949, the trumpet player Nash Hernandez founded an all-Hispanic band to play country and tejano music, opening the doors for many other Hispanic artists. The Nash Hernandez Orchestra, now led by Nash's son Ruben, carries on the tradition today, welcoming members also from other parts of the world.

In the same era, the Chitlin' Circuit—a circuit of bars spread around the US where African American musicians, actors, artists, and intellectuals were free to express themselves and perform during racial segregation—was thriving thanks to the Eastside music halls, which hosted artists like B.B. King and Ray Charles. Their legacy is still palpable and was a crucial part in establishing the city's music identity.

In the 1950s, rock and roll arrived in Austin. It was one of the first stops on a young Elvis Presley's tour in the early days of his career.

In the 1960s, a girl entered a bar called Threadgill's Tavern barefoot and asked to sing. When Kenneth Threadgill—a Texan folk singer who played with Hank Williams and was considered "the father of Austin's country music" for having discovered and supported musicians who played at his bar—heard her sing, he immediately saw her talent and decided to take her under his wing. Her name was Janis Joplin.

At the end of the 1970s, Austin was a sleepy town of 200,000 people mainly divided into two social groups that were constantly at odds: conservative white cowboys and liberal hippies with long hair and tie-dye clothes. Eddie Wilson was the one to sow peace between them. He, along with Willie Nelson, founded the Armadillo World Headquarters, which was loved by both sides. It wasn't long before you could see young people with long hair wearing cow-

boy hats and cowboys smoking cigarettes that didn't necessarily contain only tobacco. Willie Nelson is also credited with having started the "Cosmic Cowboy" movement and launching Austin as the "Live Music Capital of the World."

In 1974, at 6A studio of KLRU on the University of Texas campus, the *Austin City Limits* TV show debuted. Each episode hosted a live show and the first guest was Willie Nelson. ACL, as it is known, is still running today almost forty years since its first show from the hyper-modern Moody Theater, and during its time, it has introduced every type of music genre that ever got its start in the US to the world.

The blues and rock guitarist Stevie Ray Vaughan made Austin his home in the 1970s and '80s. There, his group Double Trouble published their debut album *Texas Flood* in 1983, an incredible success that was followed the next year by the masterpiece *Couldn't Stand the Weather*. The guitarist's career, however, came to an abrupt end after a tragic helicopter accident in 1990 while touring with Eric Clapton. A statue in his honor stands on the edge of Lady Bird Lake.

With the 1970s came Austin outlaw country, a movement that started in contrast to the clean production and limiting structure of Nashville Sound. Then in the 1980s, there was punk; in the 1990s, garage band; and with the new millennium, the start of the era of festivals: SXSW, ACL, and Fun Fun Fun Fest. Millions of music lovers descend on Austin throughout the year to attend them.

South by Southwest, or SXSW, is an annual convergence of film, interactive media, festivals, and music conferences organized jointly that takes place in mid-March. It is the largest festival of its kind in the world.

From the psychedelic tradition of the 1970s and bands like Roky Erickson's 13th Floor Elevators came the 2000s new wave of expanded sounds, synth and sitar, thanks to the band The Black Angels, which organizes the Austin Psych Fest every year, now called Levitation.

The new millennium also revived the big energy of the Texan city. Many bands now find fertile ground in the increasingly gentrified neighborhoods of Austin, although the spike in rent and the push for real estate expansion is becoming a problem for hundreds of live clubs that dot the city, threatening to evict or shut them down.

The statue in memory of Stevie Ray Vaughan on Lady Bird Lake

The stage at Austin City Limits Music Festival in 2018 in Zilker Park

1866 Scholz Garten, founded by August Scholz, opens.

1974 With Willie Nelson as guest, the first episode of *Austin City Limits* is recorded at KLRU studio 6A.

1972 Willie Nelson plays at Armadillo World Headquarters.

1987 In March, the first edition of the SXSW performing arts festival is held.

The city council establishes the Austin
Music Commission to preserve and
consolidate the city's music industry,
which brings in an average of
$1.8 billion annually.

1988

By official act, Austin is declared
by its own city council
as the "Live Music Capital
of the World."

1991

The first Austin City Limits Music
Festival, organized by the television
show of the same name,
is hosted at Zilker Park.

2002

Influential blues guitarist
Stevie Ray Vaughan dies while
touring with Eric Clapton.

1990

Gibson Guitar brings the
GuitarTown project to Austin,
placing thirty-five giant guitars
around the city.

2006

Map of Austin

1 **Moody Theater**
310 West Willie Nelson Boulevard.

2 **Threadgill's Old #1**
6416 North Lamar Boulevard (no longer in existence).

3 **Scholz Garten**
1607 San Jacinto Boulevard.

4 **The Soap Creek Saloon**
Bee Cave Road (no longer in existence). Although it has been razed for new condominiums, the Soap Creek Saloon was the legendary haunt of outlaw country musicians, such as Townes Van Zandt and Waylon Jennings.

5 **KLRU's Studio 6A**
2504 Whitis Avenue B.

6 **Broken Spoke**
3201 South Lamar Boulevard.
Opened in 1964, it is a historic venue where you can hear honky-tonk and country music, where Dolly Parton and Kris Kristofferson have played.

7 **Antone's**
305 East 5th Street.
Founded in 1975 by Clifford Antone, Antone's is an iconic blues venue where Stevie Ray Vaughan first found footing.

8 **Armadillo World Headquarters**
525 1/2 Barton Springs Road (no longer in existence).

9 **Liberty Lunch**
405 West 2nd Street (no longer in existence). Like the Armadillo, over the years, it has provided a place where members of any group or subculture could feel comfortable with others while listening to the same music.

10 **The Hole in the Wall**
2538 Guadalupe Street.
In business since 1974, the Hole in the Wall has remained the Austin music scene's go-to club for generations of up-and-coming bands, established touring artists, and famous rock stars.

11 **Waterloo Records**
600 North Lamar Boulevard.
Opened in 1982, it has been voted the best independent record store in the country and frequently hosts live shows.

12 **Stevie Ray Vaughan Memorial**
210 Ann and Roy Butler Hike and Bike Trail.

13 **Victory Grill**
1104 East 11th Street.
The nightclub was part of the Chitlin' Circuit and hosted famous African American artists, such as Bobby Bland, Clarence "Gatemouth" Brown, W.C. Clark, and B.B. King when Austin was legally segregated.

The historic marquee of Antone's

SOAP CREEK Saloon

2

5

WATERLOO

LIBERTY LUNCH
AUSTIN, TEXAS

10

3

4

11

8

ARMADILLO WORLD HEADQUARTERS Concert Hall

13

9

1

7

12

Victory Grill
Nourishing the Soul Since 1945

6

BROKEN SPOKE

Chicago

Chicago boasts a musical heritage that has left an indelible mark on American culture. At the beginning of the twentieth century, the Windy City was an important incubator of jazz music. Musicians migrated north from New Orleans to join Chicago's vibrant music industry and stand atop its busy stages. The growing demand for entertainment led to the birth of nightlife districts: Uptown, Milwaukee Avenue (between today's Madison Street and Pulaski Road), and South Side. These districts were brimming with restaurants, amusement parks, discos, cinemas, and dance halls that offered artists the chance to show their stuff.

Pianist Jelly Roll Morton, one of the earliest jazz musicians, began to play in Chicago in 1912. He and cornet player King Oliver, another pioneer of the genre, helped make Chicago the heart of American jazz. Oliver was the one who would bring his friend Louis Armstrong to the city. He then moved from New Orleans to play in King Oliver's Creole Jazz Band. It was during this time that he wrote his first great success, "West End Blues," recording some parts with Earl "Fatha" Hines.

Cloud Gate by Anish Kapoor, the famous "Bean" in the heart of Millennium Park in Chicago

A copy of "West End Blues"
by Louis Armstrong, 1926–1928

For all the 1920s, jazz echoed throughout the city's bars. On the South Side, some places catered to clients of mixed races, making jazz music an integral part of a still segregated city.

After World War II, Club DeLisa carved out a place in music history thanks to Sun Ra, who began his career as a substitute pianist in the rooms of the nightclub. Sun Ra founded the revolutionary group Arkestra, a pioneer of Afrofuturism with a charac-teristic sound that blended African American traditions and African rhythms. The Beehive in Hyde Park, on the other hand, hosted many talented musicians, including singers Johnny Hartman and Nat King Cole, both from the South Side.

But no musical genre is as closely identified with the city of Chicago as the blues. Originating in the rural South, the blues arrived in Chicago with the Great Migration of

Black people to the city. Big Bill Broonzy, Tampa Red, and Blind Lemon Jefferson led the way, defining the sound and themes of Chicago blues. Memphis Minnie, Memphis Slim, and Sonny Boy Williamson arrived in the North in the 1930s, and by the end of World War II, the city had a vibrant and nationally influential blues scene. The more famous musicians came from the South, like Muddy Waters, Howlin' Wolf, and composer, interpreter, and producer Willie Dixon. All three, along with others, created a powerful mix of Southern folk music, electronic instruments, and urban themes that would go on to characterize Chicago blues.

European tours organized by Willie Dixon in the 1960s introduced the genre to the old continent, and the Rolling Stones decided to make the pilgrimage to Dixon's Chess Records studio to record their album *12x5*. Blues, like jazz, became very popular with white audiences, especially among university students who were often themselves musicians, like Benny Goodman and Muggsy Spanier.

Even the earliest performers of Chicago gospel came from the South. Pianist Thomas A. Dorsey, the "father of gospel music," grew up in Georgia before moving to Chicago, where in 1932 he became

Phil Chess, founder of Chess Records, left, with Etta James and record producer Ralph Bass

the music director for the Pilgrim Baptist Church. There he formed a choir that included Mahalia Jackson, whose recordings are considered foundational to gospel.

Soul, on the other hand, is the term used for the nonreligious offshoots of gospel style that rose to fame in the 1950s and '60s with artists like Betty Everett and Etta James, who combined the sound of holy music with lyrics about feelings and events of daily life.

Willie Dixon

The musical TV program *Soul Train* was the first to prominently introduce African American culture. Established in 1970 from the idea of host Don Cornelius, the show initially went on air on the local TV station WCIU-TV five afternoons a week. Designed to look like a nightclub, the show hosted a wide variety of musical artists and dancers. Intrigued by the local success of the program, George Johnson, President of the Johnson Products Company (a manufacturer of hair products, including the famous line of Afro Sheen products), sponsored the transmission of the show in 1971, inserting it into national programming. The success of *Soul Train* reflected the rise and popularity of soul and funk music and spread African American culture across the US by presenting an optimistic and vibrant image of the music.

In 1977, DJ Frankie Knuckles moved to Chicago to become the music director of a new venue located inside a former factory in the West Loop, called the Warehouse, where African Americans, Latinx, and gays could meet to dance in a space free from racism and homophobia. Here Frankie Knuckles, who played a creative mix of disco, funk, and gospel songs with synthesizers and drum machines, sparked a new genre, whose name comes from the venue: house.

This new style, characterized by four-four time, a dance beat mixed with drum machines and harmonic refrains, soon spread throughout the South Side.

By the time Knuckles left the club in 1983, house music was being broadcast regularly on the radios of Detroit, New York, and London, and soon the rest of the world.

But Chicago was not only the city of jazz and blues. It also contributed enormously to the new hip-hop scene, with artists like Common, Kanye West, Chance the Rapper, and Noname, whose style combines socially aware lyrics and innovative production techniques.

It was also the home to great bands like Smashing Pumpkins, Rise Against, Wilco, OK Go, and Whitney, who keep the Chicago flag proudly flying among other great music cities around the world.

1915 Jelly Roll Morton records "Jelly Roll Blues," one of the first jazz compositions to be published.

1928 Mahalia Jackson is invited by Prince brothers, Wilbur and Robert Johnson, along with Louise Lemon, to form Chicago's first gospel group, the Johnson Singers.

1921 Benjamin "Benny" Goodman makes his professional debut at the Central Park Theatre on Chicago's West Side at only 13 years old.

1930 Lester Melrose begins working with the RCA Victor/Bluebird, Columbia, and Okeh labels. Throughout the decade he would have a near monopoly on the Chicago blues market.

1922 A 21-year-old Louis Armstrong follows his mentor, King Oliver, to Chicago to play in the King Oliver Creole Jazz Band.

1935 Fifteen-year-old Nat King Cole wins a Battle of the Bands at the Savoy Ballroom and leaves school to pursue music.

1927 Eighteen-year-old Gene Krupa is hired as a member of Thelma Terry and Her Playboys, the first major American jazz band led by a woman.

1941 John Cage moves to Chicago to teach at the Chicago School of Design and the University of Chicago.

After a divorce, Dr. Donda West moves to Chicago with her three-year-old son, Kanye.

On June 20, *The Blues Brothers*, the quintessential Chicago movie, is released in US theaters.

1980

Willie Dixon becomes a full-time employee of Chess Records as a producer, talent scout, musician, and songwriter.

1951

While a journalism student at Northwestern University, Steve Albini founds the punk band Big Black.

1981

The Rolling Stones record in the US for the first time at Chess Records studio in Chicago.

1964

After meeting in a guitar store, Billy Corgan and James Iha make their live debut at Chicago Twenty One; it's the first Smashing Pumpkins concert.

1988

After a European tour, Rick Nielsen and Tom Petersson start Cheap Trick together with drummer Bun E. Carlos.

1974

Uncle Tupelo breaks up when Jay Farrar leaves the band and forms a new one, Son Volt; the remaining members continue under the name Wilco.

1994

Map of Chicago

1 Chess Records
2120 South Michigan Avenue.

2 Muddy Waters' House
4339 South Lake Park Avenue.

3 Soul Train Studio
141 West Jackson Boulevard (no longer in existence).

4 Vee-Jay/Brunswick Records
1449 South Michigan Avenue (no longer in existence).
Before Motown, Vee-Jay was America's leading African American–owned record company.

5 One-Derful Records
1827 South Michigan Avenue (no longer in existence).
George and Ernie Leaner ran one of the most successful African American–owned labels of the 1960s. Home to great R&B and gospel artists, it hosted the first studio recording of the future Jackson Five.

6 Forum Hall
318–324 East 43rd Street.
Built in 1889, it is the oldest wood-floored ballroom in Chicago.

7 The Sunset Cafe
315 East 35th Street (no longer in existence).
Later renamed Grand Terrace Cafe when Al Capone bought a 25 percent stake, this jazz club has been one of the most important venues in the city's musical history.

8 Nat King Cole's Flat
4023 South Vincennes Avenue.
In 1923, when he was four years old, the Coles moved into this three-room apartment.

9 Louis Armstrong's house
421 East 44th Street.
Armstrong lived in this gray stone house with his second wife, Lil Hardin Armstrong, also a musician.

10 Parkway Ballroom
4455 South King Drive.
It was the successor to the Grand Terrace between 1940 and 1974.

11 The Green Mill
4802 North Broadway.
Opened in 1907, the Green Mill is America's oldest jazz club and was a frequent haunt for Al Capone and his gang.

12 The Warehouse
206 South Jefferson Street.

The facade of The Green Mill

On pages 94–95
The Blues Brothers, Dan Aykroyd and John Belushi

Salvador, Bahia

With a population of nearly three million, Salvador is the third-largest city in Brazil. Capital of the state of Bahia, it moves to the rhythm of music, which it successfully uses to convey a great sense of social cohesion within its rich multicultural reality. Home to famous composers, Salvador has been the cradle of many musical genres, as well as the birthplace of the "trio elétrico," a truck with a high-powered sound system used as a mobile stage for large outdoor performances. But Salvador is best known for the Bahian Carnival, the largest parade in the world, during which more than two million people celebrate for an entire week in the streets, avenues, and squares, dancing the axé, an Afro-Brazilian rhythm. It is estimated that each year this huge event generates a financial boost of nearly two hundred and fifty million dollars. The Bahian Carnival has, in fact, been responsible for promoting the local music industry on an international scale.

Bahia's influence on Brazilian popular music has been overwhelming: the seeds of every creative and cultural revolution or innovation was planted in Bahia and then moved through Rio de Janeiro before reaching the rest of the world. The two oldest styles of samba—samba de roda and chula—were brought to Bahia by Bantu slaves and developed on its sugarcane plantations. Many of Brazil's most important popular musicians are Bahians: Joao Gilberto, Caetano Veloso, Gilberto Gil, Brazilian rock pioneer Raul Seixas, the great Dorival Caymmi, and the Novos Baianos, who made the

famous *Acabou Chorare* in 1972, considered one of the most influential albums of Brazilian music ever.

The reasons behind this cultural and musical richness are rooted in Salvador's unique multiculturalism: a city that is both province and capital and that has captured the best of everything that has passed through and landed in its immense bay over the centuries. It was here that the

A dance group in costume for Carnival

mix of indigenous, African, and European cultures reached peak richness as this was where the Portuguese and indigenous people first met, the start of a process that would lead to the birth of Brazil.

Also important are the musical ties with other Caribbean countries, for example, Jamaica for reggae and Cuba for African influence: the common roots of the two peoples, a mixed cultural heritage, predominantly African and Iberian, have led the two countries to develop similar experiences, from which artists of great musical and cultural relevance have emerged.

But the greatest musical movement born in Bahia is undoubtedly Tropicalismo. By the end of the 1960s, the entire Western world was going through a cultural shift: the United States was caught up in the war in Vietnam, while young people were joining the hippie movement and advocating ideals of peace and free love.

In Brazil, pop culture went through a drastic upheaval when the people's democratically elected president was dismissed by the military, which, soon after taking control, censored it and froze certain types of artistic production, especially those it considered hostile to the regime.

At the same time as this political upheaval, rock music was beginning to spread from the United States to the rest of the

Carmen Miranda

world, even Brazil. Many Brazilian artists, however, critical of the US government's role in supporting the dictatorship, saw this penetration as an invasion and a

From left, Caetano Veloso and Gilberto Gil in concert

threat to Brazilian culture and organized protest marches against the electric guitar, considered the symbol of US imperialism. Musicians like Elis Regina, Jair Rodrigues, Gilberto Gil, Edu Lobo, and Zé Ketti participated.

It was in this belligerent climate that Caetano Veloso, one of the most famous Brazilian singers of the time, decided to perform with the Beat Boys at the Festival de Música Popular Brasileira with the song "Alegria, Alegria," a song that mixed traditional Brazilian rhythms with the rock style of electric guitar. Veloso, who claimed to have been enlightened as an artist by The Beatles' *Sgt. Pepper's Lonely Hearts Club Band*, had heavily criticized the march against electric guitars and with his provocative performance intended to revive Brazil's long cultural tradition through the elements that had always characterized it: internalization and reconstruction of outside influences from a local perspective as opposed to closure. Gilberto Gil, one of the musicians who took part in the march, was convinced by Veloso's proposal and played a rock version of his song "Domingo No

Parque." These performances marked the beginning of Tropicalismo, a fusion of the rebellious rock and roll of the United States with the native rhythms of traditional Brazilian music. The movement takes its name from "Tropicália," a song by Veloso featuring a blend of African rhythms, Anglo-Saxon guitars, and pop-rock percussion whose lyrics describe this fusion of people and cultures into a single multicultural, Brazilian identity. Veloso, along with other musicians, including Gilberto Gil, also released an "album manifesto" of the movement: *Tropicália: ou Panis et Circencis*.

Tropicalismo redefined Brazilian music, which was at the time dominated by bossa nova, a mix of jazz and samba, with a completely new style: tropicalistas mixed psychedelia with maracatu, samba, pop, and capoeira.

The movement, however, was more than just a musical revolution: necklaces, dresses, and makeup were used to reject the era's norms of masculinity and morality. Visual influences, ranging from Brazilian icon Carmen Miranda to Andy Warhol's pop art, pointed to exaggerated, colorful, and flashy imagery. Tropicalismo served as a bridge to the hippie counterculture in Brazil, which saw the spread of peace symbols, long hair, and brightly colored clothing.

Tropicalismo's critical attitude also took the form of a real political stance: for example, a song by Veloso, "É Proibido Proibir," lashed out in a very direct way against the dictatorship's censorship. Tropicalist performances and shows fueled the fire of resistance against the military regime. In response, in late 1968, Caetano Veloso and Gilberto Gil were awakened by police and taken to jail. Arrested without charge, they were held in solitary confinement for months and finally exiled to England, where they remained until the early 1970s, when they were allowed to return to Brazil.

Tropicalismo was a cry for freedom in the midst of the repressive culture of the most tyrannical regime in Brazil's history. Although military censorship immediately suppressed it, its short life ignited the fuse of the counterculture that would eventually end the dictatorship and change Brazilian music forever.

1968 Caetano Veloso, Gal Costa, Gilberto Gil, Nara Leão, Os Mutantes, and Tom Zé publish *Tropicalia ou Panis et Circensis*, an album manifesto of the tropicalismo movement.

In the historic palace of the Casarão dos Azulejos Azuis, the Cidade da Música da Bahia museum opens. **2021**

The Ilê Aiyê, pioneers of the Bloco Afro, a live street band that performs during carnival, is formed in the Liberdade neighborhood. **1974**

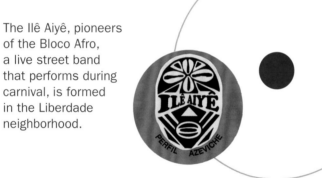

Salvador is declared a UNESCO Music City. **2015**

In Capelinha, Roque Cezar decides to put together a group that mixes samba, reggae, and regional Bahia rhythms: Harmonia do Samba, one of the best-known Brazilian groups in the world. **1993**

The Ara Ketu, a Bloco Afro socially committed to fighting racism and discrimination, is founded. They were the champions of Salvador's carnival in 1981, 1982, and 1983. **1980**

Map of Salvador, Bahia

1 **Cidade da Música da Bahia**
Praça Visc. de Cayru, 19—Comercio, Salvador.
Immersive museum where you can discover and feel part of one of the world's richest musical heritages.

2 **Fundação Casa de Jorge Amado**
Largo do Pelourinho, 15—Pelourinho.
Foundation dedicated to one of Salvador's most famous and beloved writers; often hosts concerts of traditional Bahian music.

3 **Pelourinho**
Historic neighborhood and heart of Salvador's music scene, with many bars and restaurants offering live music performances.

4 **Casa da Felicidade Arte & Música & Gastronomia**
R. da Paciência—Rio Vermelho, Salvador.
This venue in the Rio Vermelho neighborhood is a popular spot for live music performances ranging from samba to forró, rock to reggae.

5 **Teatro Castro Alves**
Praça Dois de Julho, s/n—Campo Grande, Salvador.
The concert hall with the largest stage in South America.

CASA DA FELICIDADE
arte, musica & gastronomia

Kingston

Kingston is a world-renowned hub of music. The birthplace of six distinct musical genres—mento, ska, reggae, rocksteady, dub, and dancehall—and a springboard for the careers of musical legends such as Bob Marley, Dennis Brown, Peter Tosh, and Jimmy Cliff, the Jamaican capital continues to have a significant impact on the global music scene. Today it boast the highest number of recording studios and most music production per capita in the world. Its sound system culture is unparalleled, thanks also to the help of the government, which has always supported the creative industries—especially music—as drivers of the country's economic growth.

The roots of reggae began at the end of the 1940s and '50s. This was a golden age for mento, a type of Jamaican folk music that predates ska, rocksteady, and reggae. Although it is often confused for calypso, a very rhythmic musical genre punctuated by vocal harmonies from Trinidad and Tobago, mento is a little less syncopated and usually plays with string instruments.

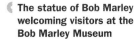
The statue of Bob Marley welcoming visitors at the Bob Marley Museum

Mento musicians like Harry Belafonte, Louise Bennett, Count Lasher, Lord Lebby, and Lord Flea generated the first wave of recording artists known beyond the island's shores.

Although the sound of the city began to shift, mento remained the sound of the rural areas until the end of the 1950s when radios because more accessible to a wider population of Jamaica. This new technology allowed families to access radio stations in Miami and the southern United States. It wasn't long before an entire generation of young people were mad for R&B. As the music of North America blended with the young Jamaican culture, the music of the island and the way it was listened to live began to change. This gave rise to two fundamental elements in the history of music in Kingston: ska and the sound system.

Before radios began to broadcast US music, American soldiers stationed on the island during World War II introduced young Jamaicans to their pop music. From the marriage of jazz and R&B with the typical rhymes of Jamaican-Afro revival, a genre that rediscovered the roots of African music, came ska, a celebratory and up-tempo sound that served as the score to the country's fight for independence from Great Britain in 1962. The first artists, like The Skatalites and The Wailers, became legends who influenced musicians of every decade

and corner of the globe, from Madness to The Specials, Sublime to No Doubt.

At that time, neighborhood parties with dancing and massive audio systems called "sound systems" were the center of urban life in Kingston. Born on the streets at the end of the 1950s, mobile speakers—complete with turntables and amplifiers—sparked a whole microculture with its own customs, factions, and leaders. Rival teams armed with heavy, 10-inch acetate discs called "dubplates" battled with music and dance to win the love of the crowd and musical control of the neighborhood.

As Jamaica moved toward independence, Rastafarian elements—like the three Nyabinghi drums—began to creep into the compositions of some musicians, with songs like "O' Carolina" by the Folkes Brothers and "Tribute to Marcus Garvey" by The Skatalites. Rastafarianism began to take form as early as the 1930s on the island as a religious and social movement, aspects that fully infiltrated the music of that time, particularly reggae.

Toward the end of the 1960s, the new genre of reggae developed from ska. Its main themes were peace, love, justice, and equality, which mirrored the ideals of the American countercultural movement of the same

▲ Lloyd Brevett of The Skatalites in concert

time period. Since the economic upturn predicted by Jamaican independence politicians never materialized, disappointment led many young artists to question the ideals of those in power through a genre that blended ska with new sounds rooted in syncopated drums and strong base lines.

Reggae and the simplicity of its structure launched a musical revolution lead by Bob Marley & The Wailers, with lyrics that dealt with sociopolitical and religious themes and spread messages of love and positivity. Songs like "Get Up, Stand Up" and "I Shot the Sheriff" made them international superstars. With them, other artists of note, such as former Wailer Peter Tosh, Jimmy Cliff, Burning Spear, Black Uhuru, Toots & the Maytals, Israel Vibration, and Culture emerged as global stars.

The producer of The Wailers, Lee "Scratch" Perry, was chosen by the legendary British punk group The Clash to produce their records, while the success of English bands like the Police and Steel Pulse, heavily influenced by reggae sounds, made the influence of the genre on the global musical landscape even more evident.

In addition to ska and reggae, another Jamaican musical genre changed the history of music: dub.

▲ **A young man posing in front of a mural on a wall at the Black Ark Studio**

Made popular by producing wizards like Lee "Scratch" Perry and King Tubby, dub is an instrumental version of reggae originally created to test audio systems. With the growing popularity and international visibility of Jamaican music, the number of music studios in Kingston increased sevenfold. These spaces for creation and their mixers were soon considered real musical instruments by sound engineers. This was the case in the living room of a small house in the Waterhouse neighborhood of Kingston. It was here that Osbourne "King Tubby" Ruddock began to infuse his music with extreme delays, deep reverbs, and bold phasing. In the hands of Tubby, the mixer became a playground with which to go crazy on FX units, knobs, and faders.

DJs would also remove the voice from records, remixing them to focus on the beat and improvising lyrics in which they boasted about their skills, praised their friends and insulted rivals. Sound familiar? When Clive "DJ Kool Herc" Campbell, originally from Kingston, moved to the Bronx, his legendary parties gave birth to the sound that we know today as hip-hop.

In the past three decades, a slew of popular music genres has evolved from Jamaican styles, including dancehall, reggaeton, and trip-hop. Today Jamaican music continues to echo around the world, whether it's through Bob's son, Ziggy Marley, who sang the soundtrack to the cartoon *Arthur*, the successful pop music of Sean Kingston, or the hybrid futuristic techno of Burial and Mount Kimbie known as dubstep.

On page 112
Bob Marley in concert

DJ Kool Herc

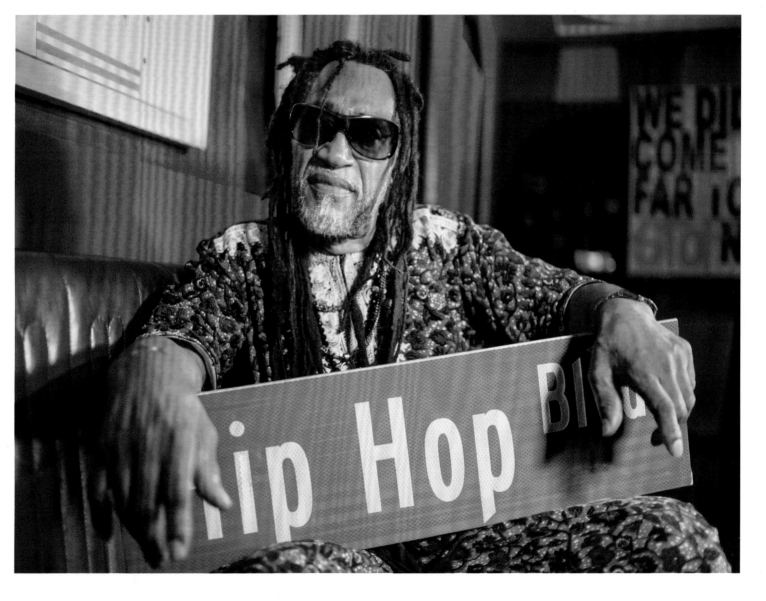

1945 Bob Marley is born on February 6.

Lee "Scratch" Perry dies at 85 on August 29. **2021**

1963 The Wailers release "Simmer Down," one of the first ska songs in history.

The release of "Rocksteady" by Hopeton Lewis gives a name to the new musical genre that would lead the way for reggae.

1967

"Say What You're Saying" by Clancy Eccles is the first successful reggae single.

The group Black Uhuru wins the first Grammy Award for the reggae genre with *Anthem*. **1985**

Dub music emerges as a genre separate from reggae, paving the way for the use of remix. **1973**

The Wailers found the label Tuff Gong, which takes its name from one of Bob Marley's nicknames. The offices of the label were in his house. **1970**

Map of Kingston

1 Black Ark Studios
5 Cardiff Crescent, Washington Gardens
(no longer in existence).
The reggae music recording studio founded
and operated by Lee "Scratch" Perry and
located in his family home.

2 Bob Marley Museum
56 Hope Road.
Opened in 1987, the museum is located
in the house where Bob Marley lived,
home of the Tuff Gong label.

3 Trench Town Culture Yard
6–8 Lower First Street, Trench Town.
Cradle of reggae music and center of many
of Marley's early creative works, Trench
Town has opened its doors to anyone who
wants to know about the birth of Jamaican
music.

4 Rockers International Records
135 Orange Street.
A springboard for many artists, it is one of
the last remaining record stores in Jamaica.

5 Beat Street
125 Orange Street.
The beating heart of Jamaican music. Ska
and rocksteady were born on this very road.

6 Alpha Institute
26 South Camp Road.
Run by the Sisters of Mercy, the school
is famous for its music classes, which
began in 1892. Jazz innovators, ska
pioneers, and reggae icons have studied
here.

7 Jamaica Music Museum
10–16 East Street.
The right place to discover archival
materials, rare music recordings, sheet
music, photographs, films, personal
correspondence, and musical instruments
that belonged to Jamaica's most famous
musicians.

The windows of the Rockers International Record Shop on Orange Street

1

BOB MARLEY MUSEUM

2

ALPHA BOYS' SCHOOL
ALPHA A GREAT JAMAICAN SUCCESS STORY

TRENCH TOWN
CULTURE YARD

3

6

4
5

7

JAMM
JAMAICA MUSIC MUSEUM

Havana

The island of Cuba and more specifically the city of Havana are considered to have had the biggest influence on Latin sound and rhythms, thanks to the contaminations, tastes, and various origins of those who made up the history of the city and the nation.

The Spaniards started it all. In the 1500s, in addition to their own sound sensibility, the earliest occupiers brought slavery to the island, subjecting thousands from Africa into forced labor. From the fusion of these two cultures came traditional Cuban music. Nothing is known about local music from before Spanish rule, except a few findings of primitive instruments like large shells, wooden horns, drums, and maracas.

African slaves brought percussion instruments and rhythms that, as was soon clear, matched European compositional techniques and especially the Spanish guitar. One of the first known

A taxi on the streets of La Habana Vieja,
one of the oldest areas of the city

songs of the time, from the second half of the sixteenth century, is "El Son de la Má Teodora" by Teodora Ginés. According to some experts, this marked the birth of one of the most famous and ancient Cuban rhythms: son, which would find success at the end of the nineteenth century.

Modern son music arrived in Havana in 1920 thanks to the efforts of legendary groups like the Trío Matamoros. Once urbanized, the genre experienced numerous changes and contaminations from popular American music and jazz, including the introduction of new instruments. Trios, typical of the traditional son, for example, shifted to bigger ensembles that included alto guitar or tres, marímbulas or double bass, bongos, claves, maracas, and later, trumpets. Singers improvised lyrics and embellished melodies while claves created the beat.

In the 1940s, musicians began to sweeten the son to pander to the tastes of the growing number of Western tourists in the nightclubs of Havana who were unaccustomed to complex African rhythms.

Another genre from its origins was the contradanza, an elegant dance successfully exported across Latin America, especially Mexico, and whose roots spread throughout European ballrooms. Developed around 1879 with the compositions of Miguel Faílde, contradanza, also called "Danzón," was originally played by the *orquesta tipica*, a band that used the structure of a military band and over time evolved to incorporate various influences, from African to French, thanks to artists like José Urfe, Enrique Jorrín, and Antonio María Romeu.

Around the same time, the rumba took hold. Largely considered a sumptuous ballroom dance, it originated as a spontaneous, improvised, and vibrant movement among workers in the ports of Havana and Matanzas. Percussion (including quintos, congas, and *palitos*, a type of clave) and vocal parts (sung by a leader and choir) combine to create a popular music that can be danced to. The rhythm is the most important part of the rumba, which was made for dancing, but was also a vehicle of expression and affirmation of identity and race for the lower classes of Cuban society.

In the 1940s, Chano Pozo was part of the bebop revolution in jazz. He played conga and other Afro-Cuban drums. The conga was an integral part of what would become known as "Latin jazz," which was invented around the same time by Cubans in New York City. Pozo, who grew up in a rough neighborhood of Havana, became a hot-

A Cuban stamp depicting Chano Pozo, from a series with the island's most famous musicians

shot percussionist on the tourist circuit in the city before immigrating to New York in 1947, where he began to play with Dizzy Gillespie, who was searching for a conga player. Their concert at Carnegie Hall that same year is considered a milestone for the birth of Latin jazz.

Fidel Castro's rise to power in 1959 sent musicians not aligned with the regime into exile in Puerto Rico, Florida, and New York; those who supported Castro were protected by the communist state, which owned record labels like Egrem. Young musicians attended music schools where they learned to play and were given full-

time jobs paid for by the state once they graduated.

Artists who were forced to leave for the US included Arturo Sandoval, Celia Cruz, La Lupe, Willy Chirino, and Gloria Estefan; many of them, especially Cruz, became symbols of the anti-Castro movement.

Political and social unrest in Cuba in the 1960s and '70s sparked a new socially aware form of music called Nueva Trova. Silvio Rodríguez and Pablo Milanés were important figures of this style, which had strong ties to Castro's revolution. It spoke of political issues but also often had lyrics that discussed the artist's emotions and intense inner and sentimental life.

With the fall of the Soviet Union in the 1990s, the situation in Cuba drastically changed. Musicians could tour abroad again and earn a living outside the state system. Nueva Trova also changed, altogether abandoning its social and political themes to focus on new songs about feelings and disempowerment.

Son and Nueva Trova are still the most popular forms of modern Cuban music and today make up the foundation of seemingly distant genres and sounds.

In the 1990s, growing interest for world music led again to fame for Cuban music,

Omara Portuondo (center), lead singer of the Orquesta Buena Vista Social Club, in concert

thanks to help from experiences like that of Buena Vista Social Club, an ensemble of Cuban musicians founded in 1996. The project was organized by the director of the World Circuit, Nick Gold, produced by American guitarist Ry Cooder, and directed by Juan de Marcos González. The name of the group comes from the club of the same name in the Buenavista neighborhood of Havana, which was a popular club in the '40s. A dozen veteran musicians were recruited to play popular styles from the age, like son, bolero, and danzón. Some of them had been retired for years, including Ochoa, Manuel "Puntillita" Licea, and Compay Segundo. This experience, documented in a famous film by German director Wim Wenders, came at a time when the Cuban economy had begun to open up to tourism and helped put the island back on the map of cultural destinations.

Ever since its appearance in the early 1990s, the timba became the most popular dance music in Cuba, rivaled only more recently by reggaeton. Timba became intimately connected to life and culture in Havana and Cuba, especially for its use of heavy percussion and rhythms that originated in the *barrios*—neighborhoods—of the city. Today it is to the city what the tango is to Buenos Aires or the pagode to Rio de Janeiro.

A group of traditional Cuban musicians

On page 122
A musician plays on the street of La Habana Vieja

1920
The son arrives in Havana, taking on a more modern and popular form.

Nick Gold, Ry Cooder, and Juan de Marcos González form the supergroup Buena Vista Social Club.
1996

1930
Don Azpiazu's Havana Orchestra performs on Broadway, giving US audiences their first taste of authentic Afro-Cuban music. The rumba craze takes hold.

La Nueva Trova emerges as a political song form in Cuba.
1970

1939
In Havana, the Orquesta Anacaona is formed.

Pete Seeger's recording of "Guantanamera" popularizes guajira music worldwide.
1966

1947
Dizzy Gillespie's Afro-Cuban jazz performance at Carnegie Hall gives Latin jazz immediate legitimacy.

The Cuban revolution brings Fidel Castro's communist government to power.
1959

123

Map of Havana

1 Cabaret Tropicana
72 e/45 y Línea del Ferrocarril, Marianao.
One of the most famous cabarets in the
world.

2 Buena Vista Social Club
4610 Avenue 31, Almendares, Marianao
(no longer in existence).

3 Plaza Vieja
The beating heart of Havana's music today.

4 La Bodeguita del Medio
Calle Empedrado 207.
A gathering place for writers, intellectuals,
and artists in Old Havana.

5 La Madriguera
Cnr Av Salvador Allende & Luaces.
Those who visit La Madrigueara
will be astonished by the musical
innovation taking place in this
artistic haven.

The counter at La Bodeguita del Medio

Pages 126–127
A dance group performing on stage at the Tropicana

Featuring COMPAY SEGUNDO ★ ELIADES OCHOA ★ RY·COODER

IBRAHIM FERRER ★ OMARA PORTUONDO ★ RUBÉN GONZÁLEZ

ORLANDO "CACHAÍTO" LÓPEZ ★ BARBARITO TORRES

LA BODEGUITA DEL MEDIO

Dublin

Van Morrison, U2, Thin Lizzy, Sinead O'Connor, The Frames, Imelda May, The Script, and Kodaline. All these musicians seem to differ greatly in genre and generation, but what unites them is the same sentiment, that which connects them to their home city: Dublin. The charming capital of Ireland might be smaller and more outlying than the great European capitals, but when it comes to music heritage, its contribution is immense.

Walking through the cobblestone streets, down Essex Street or Crown Alley, is like going to a concert. The sounds spill out of the pubs and onto the streets, from the windows of apartments and the corners of squares full of musicians playing for passersby. Rock, pop, indie, blues, jazz, folk music—there's no genre that doesn't fill the city's streets, which teems with hundreds of musicians and buskers. In Dublin, music is considered a life-giving experience that bonds all people.

Ha'penny Bridge connects the two
banks of the River Liffey in Dublin

The Corrs

worked with international artists like Bob Dylan and Willie Nelson. Their songs have influenced fellow Irish artists, including Sinéad O'Connor, who combined *sean-nós* (old style) singing with a more rock look and sound; The Corrs, who grew up playing traditional music; and London-based The Pogues, whose wild and lively version of *The Irish Rover*, recorded with The Dubliners, is a classic. There's no set formula for starting a traditional jam session in a Dublin pub. Musicians can show up and play for however long they want. Usually all they need is a few chairs and a couple of patrons, the start of a crowd that will fill the bar until closing time. The main instruments are the fiddle, the flute (or tin whistle), traditional bodhrán drum, accordion, Uilleann pipes, and the guitar.

Pubs have always been the beating heart of the city's music scene. The International Bar is where Ronnie Drew met Luke Kelly for the first time and started The Dubliners (you can still find them there a few evenings playing together). Whelan's has been supporting and nurturing rock and indie artists for more than twenty years; Ed Sheeran even attributes his success to his first few concerts at the venue. Punk and rockabilly lovers head to The Thomas House, and metal fans can be found at Bruxelles.

Irish folk music has a vibrant, upbeat rhythm that first touches the heartstrings and then gets the foot tapping in traditional dances. Rooted in the history and culture of Dublin, folk music transcended the city limits thanks to the music of The Chieftains and The Dubliners, who are today embraced by residents as legendary folk heroes. The two bands introduced the world to the traditional music of Ireland and have

In 1976, Larry Mullen Jr., then a fourteen-year-old student at Mount Temple Comprehensive School in Dublin, put an ad on the school bulletin looking for musicians for a new band. Five boys answered and they met to play for the first time in Larry's kitchen. With him on the drums, there was Paul Hewson ("Bono") as lead vocals; David Evans ("The Edge") and his brother Dik on guitar; Adam Clayton, friend of the Evans brothers, on bass; and Ivan McCormick, who left the band shortly after with Dik. The four remaining became U2 in the summer of 1979. They played a series of afternoon shows on the weekends at Dandelion Market in Dublin. The next year, the first edition of the their debut album, *Boy*, which had a post-punk sound and lyrics that explored issues like sexuality and mental health, sold 200,000 copies and kicked

Philip Lynott outside Bruxelles in Harry Street, Dublin

off their stellar career, which never lost sight of its political and social activism.

Civic engagement is also part of the career of Bob Geldof, another famous Dubliner. In the 1970s, he and his band The Boomtown Rats—a standout in the Irish new wave and post-punk scene—was one of the first to tell the story of a school shooting in the US, told from the perspective of the perpetrator, in the song "I Don't Like Mondays," the sentence the shooter used to justify her actions. In the following decade, he was the creator and promotor—along with Midge Ure, frontman of Ultravox—of two of the biggest music charity events in history, which raised funds for the people of Ethiopia suffering a disastrous famine between 1983 and 1985: the creation of the supergroup Band Aid in 1984 to record the Christmas single "Do They Know It's Christmas?" and the organization in July 1985 of Live Aid, a global mega-concert performed simultaneously on two stages in London and Philadelphia, where the biggest artists of that time played, including Queen, whose performance entered rock music history, and Phil Collins, who chose to play in both locations by boarding a Concorde to get from one show to the next.

In the new millennium, Fontaines D.C. carried on the torch of the Dublin post-punk bands. The members of the group met in 2014 while attending a college for music and bonded over their love of poetry. Their sound and attitude are inspired by that of Sinéad O'Connor, whereas Albert Camus and John Williams are cited as literary references for their lyrics, which are often in Gaelic.

With this mix of venues, sounds, and experiences, Dublin undoubtedly claims the title of global capital of music.

The Fontaines D.C. on stage

1963

The Beatles go to Dublin for the first time for two concerts at Adelphi Cinema on Middle Abbey Street.

1979

The Boomtown Rats publish "I Don't Like Mondays."

1976

Thin Lizzy tops the Irish charts with "The Boys Are Back in Town," the single that will make them known worldwide.

1983

Thin Lizzy plays at the Royal Dublin Society on their farewell tour. The concert is broadcast simultaneously on two national radio stations.

A guest on the celebrated American TV show *Saturday Night Live*, Sinéad O'Connor sings her own version of Bob Marley's "War" while ripping up a photo of Pope John Paul II on the air in protest against the abuse of minors by clergymen.

1992

The Boomtown Rats play together for the last time at Self Aid, a concert to raise awareness of Ireland's unemployment problem.

1986

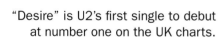

Westlife enters the Guinness Book of World Records for the most concerts held in different cities in the shortest time, playing in five different cities in thirty-six hours.

2002

"Desire" is U2's first single to debut at number one on the UK charts.

1988

After being noticed by the popular British music program *Later... with Jools Holland*, Imelda May wins Best Irish Female Musician at the Meteor Awards, Ireland's highest national music award.

2009

Map of Dublin

1 The Cobblestone
77 King Street North.
Described as "a drinking pub with a music problem," the venue offers some of the best traditional music sessions in town seven nights a week.

2 Vicar Street
58–59 Thomas Street.
A multi-award-winning and beloved venue, it has hosted distinguished musicians like Paul Simon, Bob Dylan, and Lana Del Rey, and The Dubliners, Christy Moore, and Paul Brady have recorded live albums there.

The Vicar Street sign

3 Whelan's
25 Wexford Street, Portobello.

4 Phil Lynott Statue
Harry Street.
Life-size bronze statue of Phil Lynott, Thin Lizzy frontman, placed outside one of his favorite pubs, Bruxelles.

5 Irish Rock 'N' Roll Museum
Curved Street, Temple Bar.
Museum tracing the history of Dublin music and bands; the building also houses recording studios and concert halls.

6 Temple Lane Studios
8 Cecilia Street, Temple Bar.
The studios where some of Ireland's top music artists have rehearsed and recorded, including Van Morrison, Rory Gallagher, and U2.

7 Claddagh Records
2 Cecilia Street.
Record store specializing in traditional Irish music, it used to be a recording studio called STS, famous for hosting the recording of part of U2's album *Achtung Baby*.

8 The Stag's Head
1 Dame Court.
Wonderfully preserved Victorian pub that dates back to 1770. Every Saturday night it hosts traditional music jams in the basement, one of Dublin's best-kept secrets.

9 Clarence Hotel
6–8 Wellington Quay, Temple Bar.
This luxurious hotel in the heart of the Temple Bar neighborhood has two exceptional owners: The Edge and Bono.

On pages 138–139
The Edge and Bono from U2 on stage at Croke Park Stadium in 2005

THE CLARENCE HOTEL

Cobblestone

Claddagh Records

VICAR ST.

1

9 5 7
6
8

2

4

3

TEMPLE
ANE STUDIO

Whelans

London

The British capital has always been a haven of unparalleled artistic and musical creation not only in the United Kingdom but in the world.

In the 1950s, when post-war reconstruction had just begun and the city's radios still played the notes of Vera Lynn's version of "There'll Always Be an England" on repeat, there was a need for a new sound among young people, one that was different, quicker, and more engaging. Inspired by the rock and roll on the other side of the Atlantic, young Londoners began to distance themselves from traditional jazz and use alternative instruments to create a sound that harked back to another US genre that they revived and modernized: skiffle.

Skiffle borrowed from American folk music, particularly blues, country, and jazz. Musicians played with real instruments and makeshift ones like the washtub bass, cigar-box fiddle, washboard, and comb-and-paper kazoo.

At the end of the 1950s, it is estimated that there were 50,000 skiffle bands across Great Britain. Some of the most famous patrons of this genre were members of The Beatles, The Rolling Stones, and The Shadows. The clubs of Soho and the 100 Club on Oxford Street made London the place to be for young musicians of the time, a place where a bit of musical training, some homemade instruments, and the right attitude could make you a superstar, like Lonnie Donegan.

Skiffle eventually led to the musical revolution that would take over in London in the 1960s. Born as a version of skiffle with rock and roll influences before transforming into another sound, beat music not only gave its name to one of the greatest bands of all time, The Beatles, but it also ushered in the era of the 1960s. The heart and soul of this time period was Carnaby Street, with its trendy clothing stores frequented by artists, models, and fashionable young people.

With bands like The Kinks, The Who, The Rolling Stones, and The Yardbirds emerging on the local scene and Carnaby fashion taking over the world, London in the mid-1960s was the center of the rock music world.

Toward the end of the decade, the rock sound gave way to psychedelia, with Eric Clapton's band Cream, Pink Floyd, and The Jimi Hendrix Experience, the band of the famous American guitarist, putting down roots in London.

It wasn't long before the sounds of London rock led to the creation of new experiences outside of Carnaby Street in other neighborhoods.

The newest scene in 1960s London was undoubtedly punk, a genre that combined fashion and harsh melodies. The Damned, the Sex Pistols, and The Clash, along with stylists like Malcolm McLaren and Vivienne Westwood, helped make punk, with

▿ Fans of the Rolling Stones wait in front of the 100 Club on Oxford Street in 1982

Front, Vivienne Westwood and Malcolm McLaren pose
in their boutique, Sex

its ripped jeans, mohawks, and scornful attitude, one of the most influential trends of
the century.

In the 1980s, London once again found
itself at center stage with post-punk.
Regency-era jackets, brightly colored

Boy George with a friend

silk scarves and over-the-top hairstyles were the uniform of choice of the army of New Romantics in the city's hottest clubs. Inspired by the eccentric dress of David Bowie and strongly opposed to the anti-fashion severity that increasingly characterized punk, New Romantic artists began to frequent The Blitz, a nightclub in Covent Garden founded by Visage frontman, Steve Strange, and assert a sense of gender fluidity with their makeup and flamboyant accessories. Those among the "Blitz Kids," as they came to be known, were members of bands that would shape the sound of the 1980s, like Culture Club and Spandau Ballet.

The 1990s saw interest move toward Camden Town, where the Good Mixer Pub became the stomping ground of new bands with refined pop sounds and lyrics that spoke of generational struggles. Blur, Suede, and Elastica, with their sometimes edgy sound inspired by Factory Records' "Madchester" and with some elements that came directly from The Beatles' pop style, they quickly ousted any other musical genre from the top of the charts and launched the era of Britpop.

But as Britpop stormed the mainstream, it wasn't long before Pete Doherty began roaming the streets of Camden in a Victorian soldier's red uniform leading his band The Libertines, becoming a major contributor to the growth of the indie-rock scene of the early 2000s. Accompanied by guitars and shaky drums, Doherty's poetic lyrics blended stories of substance abuse with classical British mythology.

As indie was in full bloom in Camden Town thanks to the music of Amy Winehouse, Razorlight, and Bloc Party, the 2000s saw the emergence of another genre in distant and more decentralized places: that of grime. Blending EDM beats (electronic dance music) and rapped lyrics that recount urban life in a violent and uncensured way, grime is unique from rap because it comes from electronic music. Rappers in the south and east of London, like Wiley, Kano, and Dizzee Rascal, most of African descent and part of the diaspora, took control of the radio waves of pirated stations in the early 2000s and spread this new genre in which they were free to share their experiences of immigration and struggle.

⟩ The statue of Amy Winehouse in Camden Market

1962 The Rolling Stones debut at Marquee Jazz Club.

1973 On stage at Hammersmith Odeon, David Bowie kills his first alter ego, Ziggy Stardust.

1967 Lee Gopthal and Chris Blackwell team up to found Trojan Records, which brings Jamaican music to the UK.

1975 Johnny Rotten, Steve Jones, Paul Cook, and Glen Matlock start the Sex Pistols.

1969 With the Apple Corps rooftop concert, The Beatles play live for the last time

1977 Marc Bolan, leader of T-Rex, dies in a car crash in London's Barnes neighborhood.

1970 Queen begins their career.

Spandau Ballet perform
for the first time
at The Blitz.

1979

With the simultaneous release
of the singles "Country House"
by Blur and "Roll With It"
by Oasis, the battle of
Britpop begins.

1995

Wembley Stadium is one of two
venues for Live Aid, the largest
benefit concert in history.

1985

As Michael Jackson performs
"Earth Song" with a children's
choir at the Brit Awards,
Pulp leader Jarvis Cocker
invades the stage,
causing scandal.

1996

In a year when rave culture
reaches its peak, Ministry of Sound
opens in London.

1991

Dizzee Rascal wins
the Mercury Prize
for *Boy in da Corner*.

2003

Map of London

1 Dublin Castle
94 Parkway Camden.
Amy Winehouse was a regular at this
lively pub, an institution that launched the
musical career of Madness.

2 The Good Mixer
30 Inverness Street.

3 100 Club
100 Oxford Street.

4 Ronnie Scott's
47 Frith Street.
The Who deafened an audience of
journalists here attending the launch of
their album *Tommy* in 1969. Jimi Hendrix
gave his last live performance here in
September 1970.

5 Abbey Road Studios
3 Abbey Road.
The world's most famous recording studios
and most photographed crosswalk, thanks
to the iconic Beatles album cover of the
same name.

6 23 Heddon Street
Another of the most imitated covers is that
of David Bowie's *Ziggy Stardust*, taken on
this street.

7 The Electric Ballroom
184 Camden High Street.
A famous concert hall, it hosted, among
others, Sid Vicious's last UK performance
and, in 2007, a surprise concert by former
Beatle Paul McCartney.

8 Berwick Street
The "golden mile" of record stores is also
the street featured on the cover of Oasis'
album *(What's the Story) Morning Glory?*.

9 Handel & Hendrix
25 Brook Street.
George Frideric Handel and Jimi Hendrix
would have been close neighbors if not
separated by two hundred years. Their
adjacent homes can now be visited.

10 Sex
430 King's Road (no longer in existence).
Malcolm McLaren and Dame Vivienne
Westwood's clothing store, where Sid
Vicious, Chrissie Hynde, and Glen Matlock
worked as clerks.

11 Amy Winehouse Statue
Stables Market, 407 Chalk Farm Road,
Camden Town.
Camden Town was the neighborhood that
Amy Winehouse called home. It honored
her by dedicating a statue to her in the
Stables Market.

12 David Bowie Memorial
464 Brixton Road, Tunstall Road.
The wall of David Bowie's childhood home
in Brixton, now a place of pilgrimage
for his fans.

13 Olympic Studios
117–123 Church Road.
Its halls and recording booths have
witnessed the presence of Jimi Hendrix,
The Beatles, David Bowie, Led Zeppelin,
Ella Fitzgerald, Queen, Ray Charles, Prince,
Eric Clapton, Madonna, Adele, Mika,
and many more.

14 Apple Corps
3 Savile Row.

15 Denmark Street
London's "Tin Pan Alley" is where
the British record industry
first developed.

Manchester

Music has always held a prominent place in British working-class cities as a vehicle for freedom, detachment, and escape from the problems of everyday life. Manchester's relationship with its music scene, in fact, can be traced back to the Industrial Revolution, when music became a cultural product with which the working classes could identify.

The photo of The Smiths posing in front of the Salford Lads Club is emblematic of this history: Morrissey, singer and lyricist, and Johnny Marr, the band's guitarist and songwriter, became icons of a generation and important figures because of their vegetarian activism, ambiguous sexuality, and, above all, their clear working-class background, with which many young people in the 1980s identified.

Manchester was already a hub for pop music well before The Smiths. In 1958, there were the Bee Gees, the three Gibb brothers from the suburb of Chorlton, destined to leave a momentous mark on disco music thanks to the soundtrack of the 1977 film *Saturday Night Fever*.

Castlefield, the old neighborhood of Manchester, now a UNESCO World Heritage Site

rived from American soul and fast tempo, over one hundred BPM, at the Wigan Casino and Twisted Wheel Club.

The city's music boom, however, arrived in the mid-1970s with the explosion of punk. It was June 4, 1976, when, on invitation from a local band, the Buzzcocks and the then semi-unknown Sex Pistols played at the Lesser Free Trade Hall. Only a handful of people showed up. Among them, however, were people who would change the city's musical history: Tony Wilson, TV host and creator of Factory Records; Peter Hook of Joy Division; Bernard Sumner of New Order; Morrissey of The Smiths; producer Martin Hannett; Mark E. Smith of The Fall; prominent music journalist Paul Morley; and Mick Hucknall of Simply Red.

That evening was the spark that ignited a fuse of epochal proportions, and in early 1977, the Buzzcocks released the EP *Spiral Scratch*, the first punk record from an independent label in history. Tony Wilson, a prominent figure in the city's music scene, at the time a presenter for the local television station Granada Television, began inviting punk and new wave musicians on his *So It Goes* show, hosting The Clash, Patti Smith, Iggy Pop, and the first television appearance of the Sex Pistols. Contact with these musical realities prompted the host to change course: in 1978, he left TV

The iconic entrance to the Salford Lads Club

In the same years, Northern Soul, a music and dance movement that emerged in northern England and the Midlands in the late 1960s, grew out of the British mod scene and was characterized by sounds de-

🔺 **Alan "Reni" Wren, drummer for The Stone Roses**

and founded his own music label, Factory Records. The term "Factory" evoked both the industrial tradition of Manchester and the New York experience of Andy Warhol. Wilson founded a company that united rigor and iconoclasm and revolutionized the world of music, thanks in part to the artists on its roster: A Certain Ratio, Durutti Column, Happy Mondays, James, and, to top it off, the Joy Division of Ian Curtis, Bernard Sumner, Peter Hook, and Stephen Morris.

With Factory Records always the center of this universe and combining rock, house, dance, electronic, and psychedelic music, in the late 1980s and early 1990s, groups such as Happy Mondays, The Stone Roses, New Order, and 808 State brought together global sounds and pop culture to create a new music scene: "Madchester" or "Baggy," a term used to refer to the baggy clothes—in particular, the flared jeans and oversized sweatshirts—worn by those who were part of it. The sounds of Madchester often involved funk and hip-hop bass, pulsing rhythmic drums, and strident indie guitars. Groups such as The Stone Roses, The Charlatans, and Inspiral Carpets incorporated psychedelia, rock and roll, acid house, and drums balanced between the cadence of The Doors and James Brown's "Funky Drummer" into their sound, defining a style that was entirely unique.

A rave at the Haçienda

Madchester's epicenter was the Haçienda, a nightclub opened by Factory Records in 1982, which, although a financial failure, was the center point for an entire generation. The venue revolutionized the city's rave and acid house scene (and also contributed to the genre's association with drug use). The Smiths walked its stage, it hosted Madonna's first concert in Great Britain, and it was the launching pad for New Order, The Stone Roses, and Happy Mondays. Although the club was closed in 1997, Peter Hook, Joy Division/New Order bassist, opened a venue called FAC251 at the old Factory premises on Charles Street that carries on the legacy. It's still in operation today.

Even during the 1990s, with Britpop raging across the nation, Manchester managed to further enhance its long-standing musical tradition and influence, giving citizenship to one of the biggest bands of the time, Oasis (brothers Liam and Noel Gallagher), and also setting itself up as a reference point for new sounds. Britpop was heavily indebted to the Madchester legacy, with Oasis bearing a heavy resemblance to The Stone Roses in their music and rival Blur originally starting out as a baggy band.

The long-standing rivalry between Oasis and London-based Blur was based not only on musical differences, but also on the social implications of the North-South divide and the supposed class connotations of each group's audience.

Along with Oasis and the whole indie scene, which included Richard Ashcroft's Verve, Manchester in the 1990s gave birth to another worldwide phenomenon: boy bands. In 1989, Manchester manager Nigel Martin-Smith wanted to create a British male vocal group modeled after the American boy band New Kids on the Block. His vision, however, was to create a band that appealed primarily to teenagers while also attracting the attention of other demographics. In 1990, after bringing together Gary Barlow, Mark Owen, Howard Donald, and Jason Orange, he placed an ad to find another singer, to which sixteen-year-old native of Stoke-on-Trent, Robbie Williams, responded. Together they became Take That. The rest is history.

1922 The British Broadcasting Company begins regular radio broadcasts from its Manchester station 2LO.

1951 Free Trade Hall, rebuilt after bomb damage, reopens as a concert venue.

The Buzzcocks are formed.

1976 On June 4, the Sex Pistols play Lesser Free Trade Hall.

1959 On November 15, Johnny and the Moondogs play in the regional finals of a TV talent show at the Manchester Hippodrome, Ardwick Green. It is the first time that the three members, John Lennon, Paul McCartney, and George Harrison, play outside Liverpool.

1971 Twisted Wheel Club closes.

Warsaw plays for the first time at Electric Circus on May 29. They will change their name to Joy Division the following year.

1977

Haçienda opens as a disco on Whitworth Street.

1982

Tony Wilson and Alan Erasmus found Factory Records.

1978

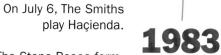

On July 6, The Smiths play Haçienda.

The Stone Roses form.

1983

Happy Mondays form.

1980

On August 18, Oasis plays their first concert at the Boardwalk Club.

1991

Map of Manchester

1 **Factory Records**
86 Palatine Road, West Didsbury (no longer in existence).

2 **The Haçienda**
11–15 Whitworth Street West (no longer in existence).

3 **The Free Trade Hall**
Peter Street.

4 **FAC251**
112–118 Princess Street, Manchester.

5 **Salford Lads Club**
St. Ignatius Walk, Salford.

6 **Southern Cemetery Gates**
212 Barlow Moor Road, Chorlton.
Another address for die-hard Smiths fans: it was the inspiration for their song "Cemetery Gates" from the album *The Queen Is Dead*.

7 **Southern Cemetery Gates**
177 Fog Lane.
The store where Liam and Noel Gallagher bought their music when they were growing up, mentioned in the song "Shakermaker."

8 **The Boardwalk**
Little Peter Street.
One of England's most legendary venues, it is known as the place where Oasis made their live debut, but it has also hosted other Madchester icons such as The Charlatans and The Stone Roses.

9 **The Temple of Convenience**
100 Great Bridgewater Street.
This bar (and former Victorian bathhouse) in downtown Manchester is mentioned in one of Elbow's most famous songs, "Grounds for Divorce."

10 **Epping Walk Bridge**
Hulme.
This bridge is where photographer Kevin Cummins took one of Joy Division's most famous photos.

USE HEARING PROTECTION

FAC51
THE HAÇIENDA

The logo of the Haçienda with the clever warning "Use hearing protection"

On pages 160–161
Noel and Liam Gallagher of Oasis read an article about The Stone Roses in *New Musical Express*

THE BOARDWALK
Manchester

BABES IN TOYLAND

WEDNESDAY
AUGUST 21
Doors Open 8.00pm

FAC 251
THE FACTORY

A BRAND NEW
INDIE ROCK+ROLL CLUB
& LIVE VENUE

COMING

SALFORD LADS
CLUB

sifters

Glasgow

Widely recognized as an important international hub of music, Glasgow is the music capital of Scotland, and after London, the second economic center for the music industry in the United Kingdom. Historically, music played a key role and still continues to be a vibrant part of city life today, so much so that it is considered by local policies to be a form of art as well as a tool for education and social integration.

The Scottish capital, which was named a UNESCO City of Music in 2008, boasts an impressive number of live music venues, from pubs to intimate clubs and major arenas, including the Britannia Panopticon Music Hall in Trongate, the oldest music hall in the world, which opened in 1857.

Scottish folk music is still an important part of the cultural heritage of the city, with its *ceilidh* (traditional dance events) and fiddle sessions, which still garner a substantial following. However, its music production extends well beyond its roots. Over the years, Glasgow has been a cradle for influential artists in different genres, including indie-rock, post-punk,

Franz Ferdinand

their return. This sums up the atmosphere that surrounds live music in the city. In Glasgow, the emotional involvement is so strong that bands find themselves playing for the best audience a musician could ask for. First opened in the 1930s on Gallowgate, Barras is just one of the many iconic places where bands go to play. The major halls include the Glasgow Royal Concert Hall, one of the best in the United Kingdom, located downtown, and the more recent OVO Hydro, on Clydeside, which is focused on the eco-sustainability of events.

In the tiny basements of pubs like The Hug and Pint on Great Western Road, and in smaller clubs of Glasgow's music community—like Stereo and Broadcast down town, Mono in Merchant City, SWG3 under the arches along the river, The Glad Cafe in Southside, the converted church Òran Mór in West End, CCA on Sauchiehall Street, and St. Luke's in East End—you can feel the teeming cultural movement of familiar faces and people who share interests and values. Many function as artistic spaces open to different disciplines, theaters, and visual arts, and they continue to be the starting point for many bands.

electronic, and pop; bands like Belle and Sebastian, Franz Ferdinand, and Simple Minds all emerged on the local scene before making their mark on the larger international stage.

When, in 2017, LCD Soundsystem returned to Glasgow to play after a long break, the group leader, James Murphy, said onstage that they specifically chose the Barrowland Ballroom—affectionately called Barras—with its famous springboard floor, as the place where they wanted to make

There are places, like King Tut's Wah Wah Hut on St. Vincent Street, whose histories have made it difficult to separate legend from truth. However, one thing is certain: countless bands of major fame walked through its doors. It was there in 1993 that producer Alan McGee signed a still unknown band under his label Creation: Oasis.

The clubs and pubs are not the only places where music history has been written. The streets as well have served as a stage for events that have become legendary: a young Gil Scott-Heron, African

American poet and experimental musician, could have walked the streets with his father, Gil Heron Sr., who played with the Glasgow Celtics in the 1950s; in April 1976, Neil Young played for passersby at the entrance to the Gordon Street train station a few hours before taking the stage at the old Apollo on Renfield Street with his band, Crazy Horse; in May 1985, The Clash played on the streets of the city up to

Billy Corgan on the stage at St. Luke's Church in 2019

Old Dumbarton Road, outside Dukes Bar; and Nirvana held a concert at the university's Queen Margaret Union at the end of 1991 and the set list, written by hand by Dave Grohl with a footprint of Kurt Cobain's shoe on it, was preserved for years in a safe at the school.

But it's not just clubs and concerts that have made music history in Glasgow. There are many bands and artists from the Scottish city who have left an indelible mark on the international scene. The soft voice of Stuart Murdoch of Belle and Sebastian, the primitive energy of Primal Scream, the melodies of Camera Obscura, the sophisticated sound of Blue Nile, the guitars of Franz Ferdinand, the electronic atmosphere of Chvrches, just to name a few, have shaped the sound of indie-rock beyond the limits of the city.

As often happened in the UK, for decades art schools were sites where alternative music scenes started and were nurtured. Edwyn Collins and Orange Juice, for example, formed at the Vic Bar School of Art; Life Without Buildings and later Still House Plants were founded in a community of art students.

Although they came from outside the city, The Jesus and Mary Chain and Teenage Fanclub were formed in Glasgow's thriving and successful scene, as were Sophie, Hudson Mohawke, and Rustie, who took their first steps toward the international dance floor with their electronic music that transcends every possible genre and category.

The sense of community is so strongly felt by musicians of Glasgow that often they are tied to their city and want to give back in some way: for example, Stephen McRobbie of The Pastels opened Monorail, one of the best record shops in Scotland; bands like The Delgados and Mogwai opened the labels Chemikal Underground and Rock Action Records and made the records of important artists like Arab Strap and The Twilight Sad; the techno duo Slam managed to get the debut of Daft Punk, signing them to their Soma label and publishing some of their first recordings.

The music of Glasgow reflects the diverse cultural landscape and rich history of the city. From its roots in traditional music to its thriving contemporary scene, the Scottish city continues to shape the sounds and world of contemporary music.

Marc Bolan of T. Rex onstage at the Apollo

On page 168
The Òran Mór

1857 Britannia Panopticon Music Hall opens on Trongate.

Sophie, a Glasgow-based electronic artist who pioneered the micro-genre of hyper-pop in the 2010s, dies in an accident.

2021

1963 The Beatles play at Glasgow Concert Hall, but the fans' screams are so loud that no one can hear the concert.

Stuart Murdoch and Stuart David, both enrolled in the Beatbox program for unemployed musicians at Stow College in Glasgow, form Belle and Sebastian.

1994

Alan Horne founds Postcard Records as a vehicle for publications by Orange Juice and Josef K. The label's motto is "The Sound of Young Scotland."

1979

An unknown band named Oasis from Manchester is discovered by producer Alan McGee at King Tut's, where they had asked to be placed on the schedule at the last minute.

1993

Dubbed "the last band to incite a riot" for a concert the North London Polytechnic that got out of control in 1985, The Jesus and Mary Chain goes wild at the Barrowland Ballroom, playing nine songs in half an hour.

1986

The Stone Roses concert at the Glasgow Green is considered one of the most important moments of live music by a band.

1990

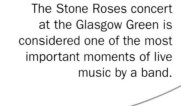

Map of Glasgow

1 **Britannia Panopticon Music Hall**
113–117 Trongate.

2 **King Tut's Wah Wah Hut**
272A St. Vincent Street.

3 **The Glasgow School of Art**
167 Renfrew Street.

4 **Barrowland Ballroom**
244 Gallowgate.

5 **Queen Margaret Union**
22 University Gardens.

6 **Monorail Music**
12 Kings Court, 97 Kings Street.

7 **Sub Club**
22 Jamaica Street.
The world's longest-running underground club, also often voted the best club in operation.

8 **The Apollo**
126 Renfield Street (no longer in existence).
From September 5, 1973, until it closed on June 16, 1985, the Apollo was the main venue for rock and alternative music in Glasgow.

The entrance to the legendary King Tut's Wah Wah Hut

5

3

8

QUEEN
MARGARET
UNION

2

Barrowland

7

1

6

4

KING
TUTS
Glasgow, Scotland

monorail
music

Liverpool

In 2001, the Guinness Book of World Records awarded Liverpool the title of "City of Pop," as the city that saw the birth of the most records that reached the top of the charts worldwide. Today it is best known for being the hometown of The Beatles and for the vibrancy of its music scene since the 1960s, following the planetary success of the "Fab Four." But well before the Merseybeat boom, Liverpool boasted a vibrant music culture thanks to its status as a cosmopolitan port city, reflecting a wealth of sounds and influences. It was the variety that brought about the founding of the Royal Liverpool Philharmonic Society in 1840, an institution that continues to be at the center of the city's cultural life.

Liverpool's sound was influenced by the diverse voices and traditions of those who settled there in the early twentieth century, especially those from Ireland, Wales, Europe, Africa, and China. Because of the importance of its port, the city became a center of entertainment and leisure with a constant demand for performances and musicians to light up the city's evenings. In the 1950s, local singers Frankie Vaughan and Michael Holliday recorded

The statue of The Beatles at Pier Head
in front of the River Mersey in the snow

numerous hits, while Lita Roza became the first woman to top the UK Singles Chart with the 1953 single "(How Much Is) That Doggie in the Window?"

The large number of entertainment venues and its openness to influences from around the world have enlivened the city with various music influences, including country, folk, and jazz. The Merseysippi Jazz Band, the longest-running band in Merseyside, Liverpool County, was formed in 1948. It played at the opening night of The Cavern Club in 1957 and still performs today. As young musicians began to play their own versions of US rock and roll, a network of clubs and dance halls began to develop throughout the city, bringing to life a new scene: the Merseybeat. This new genre, unique for its use of the guitar as the lead instrument and catchy melodies sung by multiple harmonized voices, helped solidify the idea of Liverpool as a music city in the national consciousness, also thanks to the success of artists such as Gerry and the Pacemakers, Rory Storm and the Hurricanes, Billy J. Kramer and the Dakotas, The Merseybeats, and The Swinging Blue Jeans. Musicians less overtly identifiable with the Merseybeat sound, such as Cilla Black—who was more pop and less gritty—also benefited from their association with the scene, achieving national fame.

In 1960, John Lennon (rhythm guitar, vocals), Paul McCartney (bass guitar, vocals), and George Harrison (lead guitar, vocals), arguably the most influential musicians of all time, formed The Beatles. In 1962, Ringo Starr replaced Pete Best on drums, whereas Stuart Sutcliffe, bassist and vocalist, had left the band a year earlier for love. Initially, their musical style was rooted in 1950s rock and roll, with influences in skiffle and African American music, as can be heard on early albums, which also included covers of US songs such as "Twist and Shout" and "Roll Over Beethoven."

But throughout its history, the group experimented with different musical genres, ranging from the songwriting of American Tin Pan Alley to psychedelic rock. From their recording debut in 1963 with a pounding Merseybeat that recalled clas-

Lita Roza

sics of American rock and roll, the "Fab Four" charted a unique course in music history, maturing their sound first toward a sophisticated and signature pop sound, written largely by the golden Lennon-

McCartney duo, and then, in 1966, to more radical and experimental sounds. From 1966's *Revolver* onward, psychedelic collages and overlays, dissonances, and surreal lyrics became a source of innovation in The Beatles' music exploded in the kaleidoscopic *Sgt. Pepper's Lonely Hearts Club Band* and the legendary double *White Album* before concluding with the more mature and self-conscious songwriting in the last of their works, *Let It Be*, released in 1970.

Their clothes, style, and statements made them one of the most recognizable icons of the twentieth century, while their growing social consciousness saw them at the forefront of the social and cultural revolutions of the 1960s. The band's musical relevance was such that many prominent artists openly claimed they owed a debt to The Beatles' music. After disbanding in 1970, all four members embarked on successful solo careers. The band sold more records worldwide than any other artist without end—an extraordinary achievement considering they played together for only seven years. The songs that reached the top of the world charts from 1963 to 1970 were collected in a twenty-seven-track celebratory album in 2000.

The city's nightlife continued to serve as a springboard for musicians, and numerous music scenes sprung up one after another on the city's stages, from new wave and indie-rock to pop and hip hop. The Cavern Club will forever remain associated with The Beatles, having hosted their stage debut on the night their future manager, Brian Epstein, was in the audience. Likewise, many other prominent bands of the late 1970s and 1980s, such as The Teardrop Explodes, Echo and the Bunnymen, OMD, The Mighty Wah!, Frankie Goes to Hollywood, and Dead Or Alive, have come to be associated with Eric's, which opened in 1976 on Mathew Street in the city center.

1990s Liverpool saw the birth of shoegazing (The Boo Radleys) and Britpop (The La's, the Real People, the Farm, and Cast). Since 2000, indie-rock groups like The Zutons, The Wombats, and The Coral have become popular thanks to Bandwagon nights at the Zanzibar Club. As a response to this traditional vocal-guitar formation, another wave later emerged led by bands such as Space, Ladytron, Clinic, a.P.A.t.T., Hot Club de Paris, and Kling Klang, which derived their sounds from post-punk and experimental music. In the 2010s, rappers Tremz, Aystar, Hazey, and Still Brickin brought urban hip-hop to prominence, characterized by lyrics with a strong Scouse accent, a slang term used in Britain to refer to people from Liverpool.

Even today, the many venues and music festivals, such as Africa Oyé and Liverpool Music Week, continue to revive Liverpool's role in the British music scene and hold its position on the music map.

❯ *On page 178*
The sign at the entrance to Eric's

❥ **Gerry and the Pacemakers onstage at the Cavern Club**

1953 On March 14, Lita Roza reaches number one on the singles chart with "(How Much Is) That Doggie in the Window?"

Liverpool becomes a UNESCO City of Music. **2015**

1961 In February, The Beatles play the Cavern for the first time. They will walk that stage more than three hundred times.

The Guild of Students, the students' union, founds the Liverpool Amateur Radio Society.

Elvis Costello receives an honorary doctorate for musical merit from the University of Liverpool. **2008**

1963 The Beatles reach No. 1 on the charts for the first time with "From Me to You."

After the Spice Girls disband, Melanie C dominates the charts with "Never Be the Same Again" and "I Turn to You." **2000**

1981 In January, John Lennon's "Imagine" tops the singles chart.

In December, Frankie Goes to Hollywood takes their third single of the year to No. 1 on the charts with "The Power of Love." **1984**

Map of Liverpool

1 The Cavern
10 Mathew Street.

2 Eric's
9 Mathew Street.

3 Zanzibar
43 Seel Street.

4 Mendips
251 Menlove Avenue.
Named Mendips after the surrounding hill, it is
the house where John Lennon lived from 1946
to 1963 with his uncles Mimi and George.

5 20 Forthlin Road
Paul McCartney's childhood home is
universally known as "the birthplace of
The Beatles."

6 Casbah Coffee Club
8 Hayman's Green.
Mona Best, mother of The Beatles' first
drummer Pete, opened this club in the
basement of her home in 1959, after
discovering clubs in Soho, London.

7 Liverpool Beatles Museum
23 Mathew Street.
The largest collection of Fab Four
memorabilia in the world.

8 British Music Experience
Cunard Building, Pier Head.
The first immersive museum dedicated
to British pop and rock music.

The historic Cavern Club

CASBAH COFFE CLUB

A UNIQUE AND AUTHENTIC
BEATLES MUSEUM

P

Eric's
LIVERPOOL

6

7 2
8 1

3

5

4

THE CAVERN
LIVERPOOL

Berlin

Although it is the administrative capital of the country, Berlin is more prominently considered the cultural hub of Germany, celebrated as a cradle of creativity and famous for its intrepid artistic spirit, which has led it through its history of rebellion, revolution, and revival. Artists and musicians continued to flock there, even during the dark period before the fall of the Wall, to tap into its growing sense of defiance and desire to run against the tide at whatever cost, a sentiment that energized some of the city's communities. The grimy, clandestine, underground bars of the 1970s and '80s became the preferred spots of controversial international stars like David Bowie, Iggy Pop, and Nick Cave, as well as politically active German punk bands like Die Toten Hosen. There, deep underground and in the shadow of the Wall, a countercultural ideology took hold that continues to find fertile ground in music production worldwide today.

The story of contemporary music in Berlin began in the 1920s when cabaret was exported from Paris to the German city, which soon clothed itself in a wild, libertine spirit. It was at the Theater des Westens that Josephine Baker, wearing only a skirt made of bananas,

The famous TV Tower in Berlin
(Fernsehturm) towering over
Alexanderplatz

183

The sign for the Berliner Ensemble

performed her immortal dance. In addition to jazz, she also danced to *schlager* music, carefree and surreal songs that would later become the infamous sound of parties and beer festivals.

In response to the "lighter" entertainment of those years, the city began to make more of an effort with musical theater. In 1928, *Die Dreigroschenoper* (*The Threepenny Opera*), written by Bertolt Brecht with music by Kurt Weill, made its debut at the Schiffbauerdamm Theater; on April 1, 1930, another icon, Marlene Dietrich, would bring another piece, *Ich bin von Kopf bis Fuß auf Liebe eingestellt* (*Falling In Love Again*) by composer Friedrich Hollaender, to the silver screen. In her performance of *Der blaue Engel* (*The Blue Angel*), the song would became a cornerstone of the city's musical history.

War, the regime, division, and finally the erection of the Wall radically changed the face of Berlin between the 1940s and '60s but did not extinguish its fervor and cultural impulse. Against all odds, deprivation and the social rift of the Cold War era gave rise to a thriving underground scene in the 1960s and '70s. It was frequented by both local musicians—for example, Tangerine Dream, trailblazers of the psychedelic sound, played a key role in the development of ambient music and ground-breaking German experimental music, later named *krautrock*—and international artists attracted to the city for its revolutionary movement, including Iggy Pop and David Bowie.

The center of this era of music, which continued well beyond the fall of the Wall, was the Hansa Tonstudio, also known as "the studio by the Wall." The roots of this famous recording complex go back to 1962, when brothers Peter and Thomas Meisel opened Hansa Records in the Wilmersdorf district of West Berlin. Eager to build their own studio, they decided in 1965 to rent the production facilities of the former

◆ **Inside Hansa Tonstudio**

The Berlin headquarters of Universal Music
The Berlin headquarters of Universal Music

Ariola Records in West Berlin's Köthener Straße and set up Hansa Tonstudio (aka "Hansa by the Wall") in 1974. Erected in the middle of a war-torn wasteland, it stood almost as a last outpost of creative freedom against the Wall next door, the world's most famous symbol of repression and authoritarian control.

Famous for its exceptional acoustics, the Hansa came to prominence in the second half of the 1970s, when David Bowie and Brian Eno holed up there to write and record significant parts of Bowie's acclaimed "Berlin Trilogy": *Low, Heroes,* and *Lodger.* It was the view from Studio 2's window that provided inspiration for the lyrics of *Heroes,* the touching story of two lovers unwittingly separated.

Berlin was also an integral part of the radical shift in Bowie's lifestyle when, in 1976, to avoid the pressures of fame in the US, he sought refuge in the Schöneberg neighborhood in West Berlin to focus on living a more simple life. He shared an apartment in Hauptstraße with his friend Iggy Pop, who was at the time focused on his albums *The Idiot* and *Lust for Life*, which Bowie worked on. Over the years, Hansa hosted artists like Brian Eno, U2, Nick Cave, Tangerine Dream, R.E.M., David Byrne, the Pixies, and Rammstein.

It's no coincidence that the fall of the Wall in November 1989 coincided with the rise of clubbing culture, which made Berlin famous around the world. The intoxicating mix of hope and hedonism in the years that followed the fall was a catalyst for underground clubs that took root in the city. Today the Berlin scene has lost the spirit of those roots, but a weekend of clubbing in the city, when evenings can last thirty-six hours and the music never stops, is an unparalleled experience.

Berghain is by all rights considered the most iconic and exclusive club in the world, thanks to the futuristic grandeur of its huge industrial space (the site of a former power plant), its mind-melting sound system, and the sheer intensity of its atmosphere. Its excesses fuel the legend of a place that can transform anyone who enters. But it's not alone; there's also Watergate, Tresor, and Zur Wilden Renate, iconic spots in Berlin's techno scene that continue to prosper amid the monumental post-industrial buildings and underground bars.

Inside the iconic Berghain

1928
Die Dreigroschenoper (*The Threepenny Opera*) debuts at Schiffbauerdamm Theater.

1974
Hansa Tonstudio opens in the production facilities of the former Ariola Records.

1930
Der blaue Engel (*The Blue Angel*) is screened for the first time.

1967
In West Berlin, Edgar Froese creates Tangerine Dream.

1976
David Bowie moves to Schöneberg with Iggy Pop.

1973
Lou Reed publishes *Berlin*, a concept album that tells the tragic story of a couple in the city divided by the Wall.

The Wall falls on the night of November 9. Nirvana, which was playing in Hanover that night, arrives in Berlin after the end of their concert to witness the momentous event.

1989

Christiane Felscherinow publishes *Wir Kinder vom Bahnhof Zoo* (*We Children from Bahnhof Zoo*), the seminal book about the lives of young people in West Berlin.

1978

Historic punk venue SO36 opens in Kreuzberg in August, with the irreverent Wall Building Festival.

U2 flies to Berlin to find inspiration for their new album, *Achtung Baby*, which they record at Hansa Tonstudio.

1991

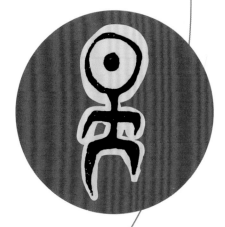

Norbert Thormann and Michael Teufele found Berghain in a former power plant between Kreuzberg and Friedrichshain.

2004

Beate Bartel, Gudrun Gut, Blixa Bargeld, and N.U. Unruh make their West Berlin Moon Club stage debut as Einstürzende Neubauten.

1980

The Next Day

David Bowie bids farewell to Berlin with his intimate ballad "Where Are We Now?" from the album *The Next Day*.

2013

Map of Berlin

1 **Schiffbauerdamm Theater**
Schiffbauerdamm 5.

2 **Hansa Tonstudio**
Köthener Straße 38.

3 **David Bowie and Iggy Pop's Apartment**
Hauptstraße 155.

4 **SO36**
Oranienstraße 190.

5 **Berghain**
Am Wriezener Bahnhof.

6 **Zur Wilden Renate**
Alt-Stralau 70.

7 **Zoo Berlin**
Hardenbergplatz 8.

8 **Tresor**
Köpenicker Straße 70.

9 **Universal Music Europe**
Stralauer Allee 1.
The European headquarters of
Universal Music.

10 **Sonntags Karaoke im Mauerpark**
Mauerpark.
The most famous karaoke spot in Europe
takes place every Sunday in the park's
amphitheater along the Wall.

11 **Monarch**
Skalitzer Straße 134.
One of Berlin's historic hidden clubs, where
you can listen to underground music
among the public housing apartments of
Kottbusser Tor.

12 **KitKatClub**
Köpenicker Straße 76, Brückenstraße 1.
Berlin's most extreme club.

13 **Clärchens Ballhaus**
Auguststraße 24/25.
A 1913 ballroom in downtown Mitte
unchanged by time, where you can twirl
among feathers and tuxedos as if it were
the turn of the last century.

14 **Das Gift**
Donaustraße 119.
A Scottish pub opened by Mogwai guitarist
Barry Burns.

The entrance to Clärchens Ballhaus

On pages 190–191
A techno DJ set at Watergate

Kotthusser Tor

Clärchens Ballhaus

SO 36

10

1

13

12

5

8

9

6

7

2

11

4

In diesem Haus wohnte von 1976 bis 1978

DAVID BOWIE
8. 1. 1947 – 10. 1. 2016

In dieser Zeit entstanden die Alben »Low«, »Heroes«
und »Lodger«. Sie gingen als Berliner Trilogie
in die Musikgeschichte ein

»We can be heroes, just for one day«

3

14

Das Gift

Paris

It is said that there are two main themes in French songs: love and Paris. In fact, the city has been the protagonist of the most beautiful songs in the history of French music. To understand where musicians' fascination with the "City of Lights" comes from, we must go back to the French Revolution. The Parisian song was originally a song of revolt. In the words of one by Delacroix, Paris was the city of "liberty leading the people," and in every corner of it one could hear new songs and nursery rhymes of seemingly childlike simplicity that often concealed harsh and direct messages that were easy to remember thanks to their form. These songs have been passed down to us through the great performers of the twentieth century: in 1953, Édith Piaf recorded the hymn of the storming of the Bastille "Ça Ira"; in 1966, Mireille Mathieu lent her voice to the liberation song "Paris en Colère" on the soundtrack of the film *Is Paris Burning?*; in 1967, Serge Reggiani evoked the French Resistance with "Les loups sont entrés dans Paris."

The typical Parisian subway sign designed
by Art Nouveau artist Hector Guimard

Édith Piaf performing in Paris

The Parisian song remains a song of rebellion of the people against the bourgeoisie, polite society, and lavishness even during the twentieth century. Its singers include Maurice Chevalier, Édith Piaf, and Charles Trenet, who spoke of proletarians and prostitutes in their songs, the former in "Prosper (Yop la boum)" in 1935 and the latter in "Milord" in 1959.

The lower classes and the cunning Parisian prankster, the accordion, bistros, and street performers, who for the first half of the twentieth century were the figures of the *chanson populo* ("folk"), would then lead to other narratives of the city in the following decades, born in the light of the new consumer society and capitalism. Two of the greatest successes of the time, "Les Champs-Elysées" (1969) and "La Complainte de l'heure de pointe" (1972) by singer Joe Dassin, are a striking example: revolution gives way to the tale of postcard landscapes, riotous mottos to ballads, class struggles to the torments of love.

Nonconformity, however, remained a hallmark of artistic and musical life in Paris, as did lightness of dress and ease in interpersonal relationships. A testament to this was the numerous cabarets, among the world's most famous nightclubs, which opened in the capital at the beginning of the last century: the Folies Bergère, which hosted the scandalous performances of Josephine Baker; the Lido, on the Champs-Élysées; Chez Michou in Montmartre, famous for its drag queen shows. And then Pigalle, the red-light district home to, among others, the Moulin Rouge, masterfully recounted by Serge Lama in his 1973 "Les petites femmes de Pigalle."

In the 1950s, music halls joined the mix. These concert halls were where singers—not dancers or dance performances—were the stars of the evening. Many of them came from abroad and wrote songs dedicated precisely to the city that had welcomed them: the Italian Yves Montand with "À Paris" in 1964, the Armenian Charles Aznavour and his "Paris au mois d'Août" in 1966, and the Algerian Enrico Macias, author of "Paris tu m'as pris dans tes bras" in 1964, joined their French contemporaries, such as George Brassens, with refined melodies and evocative lyrics.

In the same years, a previously ignored neighborhood was transformed into the gathering place of the city's artists and intellectuals: at the Café de Flore, on the Left Bank, it was not unusual to run into Jean-Paul Sartre, Simone de Beauvoir, Jacques Prévert, or Pablo Picasso, as well as musicians who embodied the new spirit of the city, the "chansonniers," as French songwriters had been called since the eighteenth century. These included Marcel Mouloudji; Juliette Gréco, who during social reconstruction after the war would lend her voice to songs such as "Sous le ciel de Paris" in 1951; and the revolutionary Léo Ferré. Gréco frequented the jazz community, and her relationship with American trumpeter Miles Davis quickly made her "the muse of Saint-Germain-des-Prés." Ferré, on the

The Moulin Rouge all lit up

Serge Gainsbourg and Jane Birkin

other hand, with his scathing wit, liked to subvert the rules of the committed chanson with "Paris Canaille" (1954), "Jolie Môme" (1961), and 1970's "Paris, je ne t'aime plus," in which he recounted a city and an era that had become alien to him.

At that time, the chanson changed again, becoming more intellectual and trying to break away from the accordion sound that had characterized the genre from its early days, which was now considered too present and stereotypical. New artists began to move from the Flore to the Deux Magots, and it was around this time that Serge Gainsbourg and the poet, writer, and songwriter Boris Vian began their careers.

Meanwhile, Saint-Germain continued to tremble under the dance moves of bebop, the more "intellectual" jazz that had just arrived from the United States, whose influence in the city's musical history continues to the present day. In the 1990s, it gave its name to one of the most famous electronic artists of the early 2000s, St Germain, pseudonym of Ludovic Navarre, who was able to modernize the local jazz tradition by mixing it with house rhythms and sounds; over time, it has continued to act as a mu-

sical hotbed, defining the typical Parisian sound, with artists such as Dany Brillant, Marc Lavoine, and Étienne Daho.

The 1970s brought with it a new revolutionary momentum from the inhabitants of the Paris suburbs, with their antisocial songs, such as Telephone's "Metro c'est trop" from 1977 or Renaud's "Marche à l'ombre" from 1980. Paris was no longer as loved as it had been in the past. Now grasped by the hands of capitalism, it was rejected, and the dehumanization generated by the drive to consume in a city that was increasingly economically exploited, turned into aggression. Having become a tourist attraction, it was disowned by the "banlieusards," residents of the suburbs in those days. At the end of the 1980s, the alternative rock of Mano Negra, Mano Solo, and Les Négresses Vertes, all of whom came from backgrounds in punk, became the mouthpiece of the growing social discomfort. Far from the Left Bank, they sang of working-class neighborhoods of gray concrete, of lives shattered by unemployment, drugs, and AIDS. "Dans la salle du bar tabac de la rue des martyrs" by Pigalle in 1990 and "Paris" by Marc Lavoine in 2001 are true portraits of the lesser-known side of the "City of Lights."

On page 200
Miles Davis and Juliette Gréco

1925

On October 2, Josephine Baker makes her debut at nineteen in the Revue Nègre at the Théâtre des Champs-Élysées.

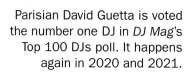

Parisian David Guetta is voted the number one DJ in *DJ Mag*'s Top 100 DJs poll. It happens again in 2020 and 2021.

2011

1929

Fourteen-year-old Édith Piaf begins performing with her father and his acrobat group as a singer.

Wolfgang Amadeus Phoenix by Phoenix wins Best Alternative Music Album at the 52nd Annual Grammy Awards.

2010

1949

Juliette Gréco and Miles Davis become romantically linked.

With his record *Clandestino*, Manu Chao, former member of Mano Negra, becomes a symbol of the anti-globalist movement.

2001

1969

Serge Gainsbourg and Jane Birkin cause a scandal with the song "Je t'aime... moi non plus."

Hip-hop radio broadcastings, such as Rapper Dapper Snapper and BA Crew, begin to spread rap in the city.

1982

Map of Paris

1 **Café de Flore**
172 Boulevard Saint-Germain, 75006.

2 **Les Deux Magots**
6 Place Saint-Germain des Prés, 75006.

3 **Moulin Rouge**
82 Boulevard de Clichy.

4 **New Morning**
7/9 Rue des Petites Écuries.
One of the city's best jazz clubs since 1981.
It has hosted Chet Baker, Stan Getz, and
Dizzy Gillespie, among many others.

5 **Père Lachaise Cemetery**
16 Rue du Repos, 75020.
Many of the great artistic and intellectual
figures of the last two centuries are buried
here, including Jim Morrison, Michel
Petrucciani, and Maria Callas.

The veranda at Café de Flore

Ibiza

I t's inevitable: what immediately comes to mind when you talk about Ibiza are its clubs and electronic and dance music scene, which have made it the ultimate destination for night owls.

But its musical traditions are of different origins. After the Spanish Civil War and Franco's rise to power, the island, until then a sleepy fishing village, became a place of refuge for artists, musicians, writers and painters seeking to escape Franco's regime and rediscover the bohemian spirit that had disappeared from the mainland. Starting in the 1960s, they were joined by hippies from all over Europe who, attracted to the relaxed atmosphere, natural beauty, and three hundred days of sunshine a year, began to converge on the Balearic Islands, turning them into an epicenter of the Flower Power movement.

In 1973, following the decline of Francisco Franco's regime, the local government decided to give tourism a boost by encouraging celebrities and musicians to come to the island for

Wham! while filming the music video for "Club Tropicana"

their vacations. They brought with them the sounds of the genre that was making them world famous: rock. Ibiza's history is full of rock-star legends, most of whom stayed in the Pikes, a hotel nestled in the hills overlooking San Antonio. Frequented by top musicians and the location of the iconic "Club Tropicana" music video by Wham!, the hotel also hosted Freddie Mercury's infamous forty-first birthday party in 1987. And it was where the singer stayed before his iconic performance at the KU Club with famed Spanish tenor Montserrat Caballé. The hotel's owner was Tony Pike, a British-born Australian, former army sailor, and inveterate playboy, who, in 1978, upon arriving on the island but after a forty-eight-hour uninterrupted party, noticed an advertisement for the sale of a *finca*, an old estate near San Antonio, that immediately caught his attention: the name was Can Pep Toniet, "Little Tony's property."

It was fate. Pike transformed the abandoned building, which had no water, electricity, or sanitation, into his five-room hotel from scratch, using a jackhammer to dig the pool and illegally connecting to a government generator for electricity.

In addition to the tourist boom, the 1970s brought the birth of nightclubs. In 1973, brothers Ricardo and Piti Urgell bought land in the port area of the city, renovated the farmhouse that stood there, and opened a club similar to the one they already owned in Sitges, giving it the same name: Pacha, a small club frequented by hippies with shell necklaces and crocheted clothes. During the 1980s, when house records with pounding BPMs began arriving from Chicago, the country house was transformed into a disco. But it was with the new millennium that the Urgell brothers' brainchild would find its final iteration as a temple of EDM—commercial, easily danceable electronic music—hosting David Guetta as the first DJ at its turntables.

Amnesia was Ibiza's first superclub. Also a converted eighteenth-century *finca* that had belonged to a fishing family for five generations, the property was sold and then leased by Antonio Escohotado, who decided to make it a nightclub. He wanted a place where people could go in the evenings and forget their troubles, indulging in a world far removed from their ordinary routine. Thus, the name Amnesia. After several changes in ownership, Amnesia in the 1980s became the cradle of Balearic house music thanks to DJ Alfredo, a resident of the club in 1983. Argentinian Alfredo played an eclectic mix

of dance music, to which he combined the hypno-indie grooves of The Woodentops, the mystic rock of The Waterboys, early house, Europop, and eccentric music of artists like Peter Gabriel and Chris Rea.

Amnesia was the location of the legendary night when British DJs Paul Oakenfold, Johnny Walker, Danny Rampling, and Nicky Holloway discovered the Balearic sound and took ecstasy for the first time in 1989. Back in their homeland, they decided to search for a sound that would help them relive the experiences of that night, creating acid house.

A performer at Pacha

The story of Privilege also began in the early 1970s. It started as a restaurant and was later expanded to include a bar and pool.

In 1979, the club was sold to Real Sociedad footballer José Antonio Santamaría, along with the creative team of Brasilio de Oliveira. Initially called the KU Club, after a god from Hawaiian mythology, throughout the 1980s it earned a reputation as Europe's premier polysexual nightclub and was compared to an outdoor version of New York's famous Studio 54.

It was there that the video of Freddie Mercury and Montserrat Caballé's performance of "Barcelona" was filmed on May 30, 1987, and over the years it hosted early live performances by groups such as Spandau Ballet and Kid Creole and the Coconuts. The club continued under the name KU until 1995, and then was christened Privilege after its purchase by José María Etxaniz.

Space (now Hï Ibiza) first opened in the early summer of 1986. The opening party included the opening of the Aguamar Water Park, located behind the club, to allow attendees to take advantage of the water slides at night. The space in its current form, however, dates back to 1989, when Pepe Roselló, already an Ibiza nightclub owner, took over the venue. The first DJs to shape the sound of Space were Alex P and Brandon Block, two British resident DJs and producers of Sundays at Space, the venue's outdoor terrace.

This outdoor terrace with the roar of planes flying over it to the nearby airport, overpowering the dance music, became one of the club's distinguishing features. Because Amnesia and Privilege had to cover their dance floors in order to remain open twenty-four hours a day following the enactment of new laws regulating noise, Space, with its two-hour daily closing time, remained one of the few places where clubgoers could experience outdoor music, and the crowd's salute to incoming flights became a ritual among patrons.

Thanks to world-class resident DJs such as Armin van Buuren and David Guetta, and state-of-the-art design and sound, tickets to Hï Ibiza quickly became one of the most sought-after tickets on the island.

The Ushuaïa Club, which opened in 2011 and was ranked by *DJ Magazine* as one of the best clubs in the world, and the Ushuaïa Tower, which opened in 2012, are both also hotels.

The Ushuaïa has a capacity of four thousand people and is one of the largest in Ibiza. A feature of the hotels is that the balcony of some rooms overlooks the dance floor, which hosts many residencies of world-class DJs, including Armin van Buuren, Martin Garrix, Oliver Heldens, Axwell and Sebastian Ingrosso, and Steve Angello of Swedish House Mafia.

Freddie Mercury and Montserrat Caballé

On page 210
Ushuaïa Tower

1973 Pacha opens as a hippie club on an old farm estate.

1983 Wham! shoots the "Club Tropicana" music video in the Pikes Hotel pool.

1988 Freddie Mercury and Montserrat Caballé choose KU Club as the location for their performance of "Barcelona."

1998 José Pascual and Lenny Krarup create the DJ Awards, held annually in Ibiza to honor international DJs in eleven categories. It is the most important event of its kind.

To celebrate the end of his fifteen years as resident DJ at Space, Carl Cox plays a nine-hour techno set. **2016**

Kylie Minogue makes a surprise appearance onstage at Pacha to sing "Can't Get You Out of My Head" during a set of her producers, Swedish House Mafia. **2010**

The Guinness Book of World Records certifies Privilege as the world's largest nightclub, with an area of nearly 70,000 square feet and a capacity of ten thousand clubbers. **2003**

Circoloco opens and immediately becomes the center of the most underground nights of the acid house scene. **1999**

Map of Ibiza

1 **Pikes Hotel**
Camí de Sa Vorera, S/N,
Sant Antoni de Portmany.

2 **Amnesia**
Carretera Ibiza a San Antonio, Km 5.

3 **Pacha**
Avenida 8 d'Agost, Eivissa.

4 **Es Paradis**
Carrer Salvador Espriu, 2, Sant Antoni
de Portmany.
Opened in 1975, it is one of the first clubs
on the island. Initially outdoors, when noise
legislation changed, it had to build a roof:
its iconic pyramid.

5 **Privilege**
Urbanización San Rafael, s/n,
Sant Antoni de Portmany.

6 **Hï Ibiza**
Platja d'en Bossa.

7 **Ushuaïa**
Carretera de Platja d'en Bossa, 10,
Sant Jordi de ses Salines.

8 **Café del Mar**
Carrer Vara de Rey, 27, Sant Antoni
de Portmany.
Opened in 1980, it is the most famous
chillout bar on the island.

The cupola of Privilege

On pages 214–215
The Dutch DJ Tiësto performing at Amnesia

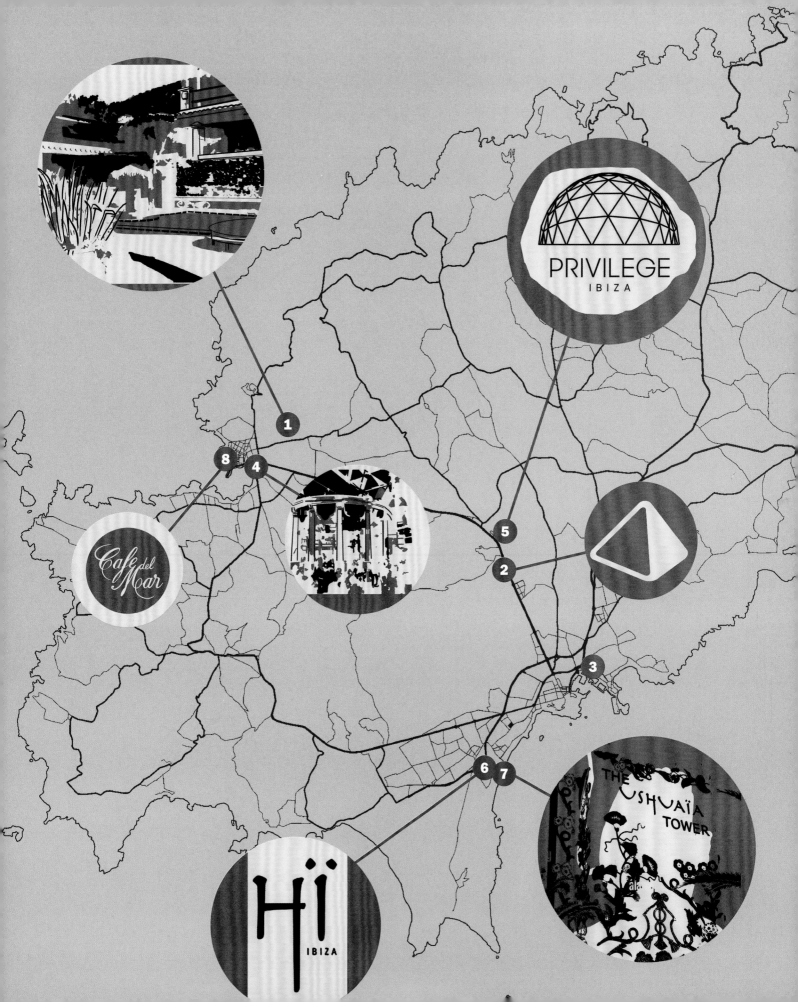

PRIVILEGE
IBIZA

Café del Mar

Hï
IBIZA

THE
USHUAÏA
TOWER

1
8 4
5
2
3
6 7

Seoul

Korean pop music flourished amid the ruins of invasions and wars: first with Japanese colonial rule from 1910 to 1945, then after World War II with the occupation of South Korea by the United States, followed by the devastation of the Korean War and the reconstruction under dictator Park Chung Hee.

During the Japanese occupation, Korea experienced rapid technological, industrial, commercial, and urban expansion. New recording and broadcasting technologies, imported under Japan's influence, made the enjoyment of music much more accessible and broadened the range of genres and styles. By the 1920s, the songs heard by city dwellers in theaters, bars, cinemas, and cafes could mix European instruments, Korean words, Japanese melodies, and early American jazz styles.

After the end of World War II, South Korea, created from the division of the Korean peninsula by the victors of the conflict, experienced another revolution: the end of Japanese

dominance and the beginning of American musical hegemony. With Korea's economy devastated by the war, soldiers stationed on US military bases were the only ones who could afford to "consume" music, which was thus played live or recorded by Koreans to suit American tastes, echoing their sounds.

Beginning in 1961, with General Park Chung Hee's rise to power, the new regime prepared a plan of growth to modernize the nation. This period saw the development of the recording industry, radio broadcasting, and television shows, the combined efforts of which led to the spread of a national style of folk song called trot, characterized by lyrics centered on the experiences of communal life in the post-war landscape and a romantic style rooted in pansori art, a genre of traditional Korean musical storytelling for voice and buk drum. Trot, however, was perceived by the younger generation as too sentimental and old-fashioned and by the regime as still too closely tied to Japanese influence. So in the early 1960s, in search of new inspiration, South Korean music found new direction in the pop music of singer Han Myeong-Sook's "The Boy in the Yellow Shirt" and the Beatles-influenced rock of Add4, South Korea's first rock band. Most of the nation, however, continued to live without electricity and therefore didn't have easy access to music. In the 1970s, the Chung Hee regime became increasingly authoritarian. The government's growing repression—the ban on long hair in 1970 and miniskirts in 1973—culminated in 1975 with Emergency Presidential Decree Number 9, which banned many South Korean records and 261 foreign songs, accused by the regime of having negative influences on national security and pessimistic content. In December of that year, Shin Joong-hyun, the leader of Add4, was arrested for marijuana possession. From then until the mid-1980s, rock music, culture, and clothing were silenced.

In the 1980s, after the assassination of Park Chung Hee, everything changed again. In the middle of the decade, South Korea was experiencing huge growth and major contradictions: the stark contrast of wealth and poverty coexisted with a military government that seemed constantly engaged in surveillance and discipline. Students and workers began to demonstrate, and the police responded violently. Meanwhile, the government's puritanical positions were being disrupted by a new art form: music videos. The rise of MTV and Michael Jackson's music videos united music, dance, and images in a modern, free language for the first time in the eyes of young people. Kim Wan-sun, the "Korean Madonna," and Park Nam Jung, the "Korean Michael Jackson," sang upbeat songs while accompanying them with choreography. The "idol" groups, as contemporary K-pop musician-celebrities called themselves, were anticipated by Sobangcha, a Seoul-based pop dance music group created by Daesung Enterprise in 1987. In the same year, massive protests from all segments of society led to the transition to democracy.

In the 1990s, South Korea was swept up in the cultural wave known as "Hallyu," which grew on the back of economic expansion, globalization, and the hosting of the 1988 Olympics in the glittering city of Seoul, shooting the nation to global prominence.

This is the period in which the birth of K-pop as we understand it today was formed. In Seoul in April 1992, former

Members of BTS onstage at the American Music Awards of Los Angeles in 2020

metal singer Seo Taiji performed with his new band Seo Taiji and Boys on a TV talent show with a rave-style swingbeat piece beginning with a long rap that, despite getting the lowest score from the TV jury, broke through to the hearts of young people. His performance paved the way for a multimillion-dollar industry that, with bands like the male quintet H.O.T., female trio S.E.S., and female quintet Baby V.O.X, the first generation of K-pop artists, set off an explosion of "idol" culture. And when the Southeast Asian economy collapsed in 1997, the government looked to the "idols," the music industry, and TV dramas to stimulate tourism and exports. In terms of sound, K-pop can be considered a hybrid of Western pop genres: R&B, hip-hop, electronic dance music, bubblegum pop, British rave, and Swedish synth pop, with touches of reggae and Latin pop, which is why it is often compared to Sibal, a Korean car from the 1950s that was assembled by reusing old oil drums and US army jeeps left over from the war. This creative hybrid blend has deeply marked South Korean culture, which, long isolated by domination and dictatorship, has survived by building a new identity through stimuli from around the world.

In 2019, Korean popular music ranked sixth among the top ten music markets worldwide. Today, thanks to the advent of social networks and the success of South Korean TV shows, the third generation of K-pop idols, like BTS, EXO, Seventeen, and BLACKPINK, have established their music on the world stage.

On page 222
The "Gangnam Style Horse Dance Stage" installed in Gangnam for photos and impromptu performances

BLACKPINK performing

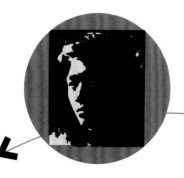

1970

Folk singer Kim Min-ki writes the ballad "Morning Dew." The song will become the anthem of the pro-democracy youth movement during the period of political conflict.

BTS is the first non-English-speaking and Asian artist to sell out Western music temples: Wembley Stadium in London and the Rose Bowl in Pasadena, California.

2020

1986

Kim Wan-sun, the "Korean Madonna," debuts with her album *Tonight*.

Rapper Psy's music video for "Gangnam Style" is the first YouTube video to surpass 1 billion views.

2012

SM Entertainment, a multinational entertainment agency responsible for promoting and popularizing the careers of many immensely successful K-pop stars, is founded by record producer Lee Soo-man.

1995

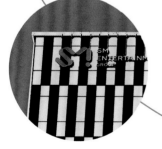

BTS, the best-selling K-pop group in history, with over 40 million albums sold, is formed.

2010

Map of Seoul

1 Ossu Seiromushi
30 Baekjegobun-ro 45-gil.
BTS member Kim Seok-jin, a food enthusiast, opened this restaurant near Seokchon Lake.

2 Lovin'her
22 Sinchon-ro 6-gil, Donggyo-dong, Mapo-gu.
One of Seoul's most famous "Birthday cafes," venues where events and parties are held to mark the birthdays of "idols."

3 HiKR Ground K-pop Experience
40, Cheonggyecheon-ro, Jung-gu.
Total immersion in the world of K-pop, including studios to shoot your own music video clip.

4 Myeongdong Underground Shopping Center
124 Toegye-ro, Jung-gu.
K-pop fan paradise with countless gadget stores, posters, postcards, albums, and records.

5 SM Kwangya Seoul Flagship Store
Wangsimni-ro, Seongdong-gu.
Opened in 2022, the store sells merchandise and memorabilia of famous artists from the SM Entertainment agency and offers interactive experiences and numerous photo opportunities.

6 K-pop Square
513 Yeongdong-daero, Gangnam-gu.
Here you can find the iconic "Gangnam Style" statue, the wall with handprints of K-pop idols, and promotional videos of the latest K-pop releases.

On pages 226–227
In the center of Gangnam, the giant bronze sculpture by artist Hwang Man-seok replicates the horse-riding gesture of the hands from the "Gangnam Style" dance by Psy

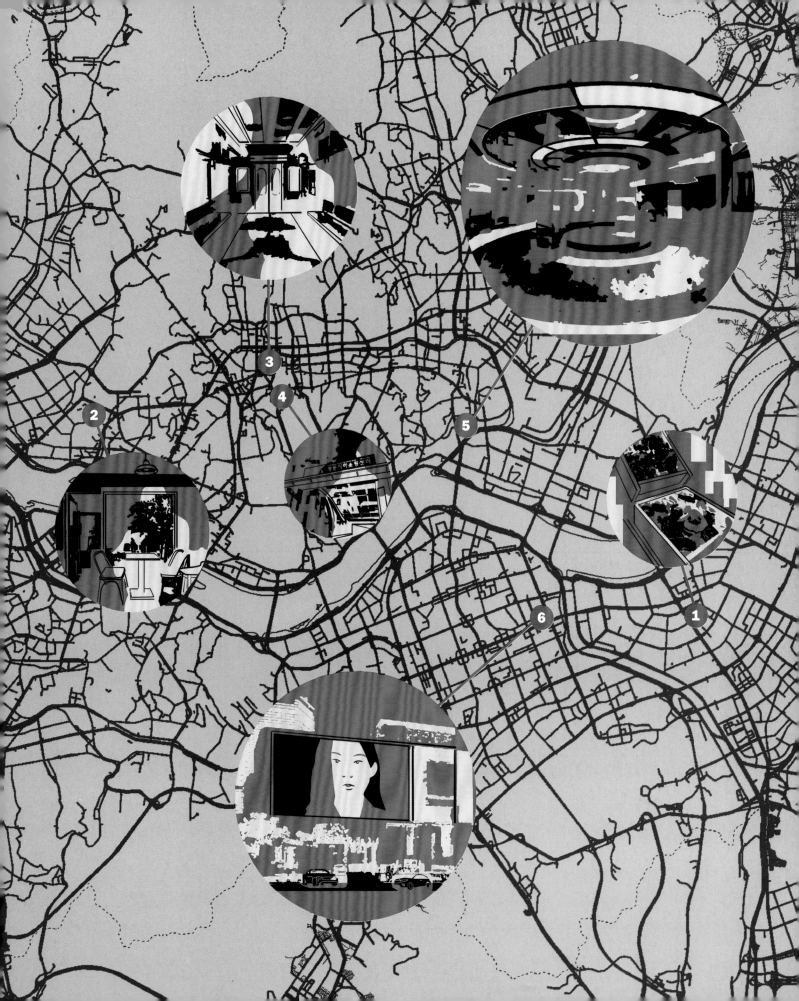

Tokyo

Between the infectious melodies of J-pop, the retro charm of Shibuya-kei, and the evocative rhythms of underground electronic music, the city has been an incubator of great talent and original styles over the years and boasts a unique blend of contemporary and traditional sounds.

One of the most popular genres of music in Tokyo—and around the world—is Japanese pop, better known as J-pop. Characterized by a wide mix of styles, from bubblegum pop to the most overt rock, J-pop has gained international recognition thanks to iconic artists such as singer-songwriter Hikaru Utada and the groups Perfume and Arashi, which have introduced the world to the versatility of Japanese musicians.

The roots of this genre can be traced back to the early Shōwa period (between 1926 and 1945), which saw the spread of popular jazz music characterized by the use of instruments previously used only in military marches and classical music. The success of the genre led to the establishment of jazz kissa, trendy cafes where people could listen to music and attend live performances.

Perfume on stage during a performance

After jazz came rock and roll, which became a craze in Japan starting in the mid-1950s. Thousands of young people, heavily influenced by the "rockabilly" music that had swept the United States and encouraged by the new postwar consumer culture, gave birth to "rokabiri būmu," the first popular youth cultural movement in post-occupation Japan. Driving this new wave were shows that took the name "Western Carnival" and were held twice a year at the Nichigeki Theater in Tokyo's Ginza district and in jazz cafes in most major cities, where people could attend rockabilly music concerts and show off their looks, based on the few images young people could find in US magazines or movies. The teenage *rokubirizoku* ("rockabilly tribe") made up the rowdy audience for the new music and were soon targeted by police and local authorities, who singled them out as delinquents. This, however, did not stop the rise of the movement, which, thanks in part to the efforts of producer Misa Watanabe of the Nabepro talent agency, nicknamed "Rokabiri Madam" by the media, became a pop and commercial phenomenon, complete with films and television programs designed specifically for the youth audience of the early 1960s.

Artists of the time, influenced by Western music, began to record new versions of American songs, adapting them to their own sensibilities. From the encounter between Western music and traditional sounds, Japanese pop music was born, which continued to expand throughout the 1970s and 1980s before exploding in the 1990s, when it began to spread outside the Japanese archipelago and take the name J-pop.

In the 1990s, another musical genre became popular in Tokyo: Shibuya-kei, named after the famous Shibuya district. Characterized by the use of electronic instruments and sampling techniques, Shibuya-kei is distinguished by a cut-and-paste approach inspired by kitsch and by the fusion and artifice of certain musical styles of the past: the sounds of the 1960s, Western pop music, and the works of Burt Bacharach, Brian Wilson, Phil Spector, and Serge Gainsbourg. Among the major exponents of this genre are world-renowned artists such as the Pizzicato Five, who fused J-pop with a mix of jazz and soul, and Cornelius (the stage name of Keigo Oyamada), considered the Japanese Brian Wilson.

In addition to the mainstream J-pop scene and Shibuya-kei, Tokyo is also home to a thriving underground electronic and experimental music scene. Artists such as Ryuichi Sakamoto and Merzbow have pushed the boundaries of sound to new dimensions, while venues such as SuperDeluxe and Ochiai Soup offer intimate spaces where artists and audiences can connect with each other over the beat of the music.

Sakamoto is one of the key figures in the city's and Japan's musical history: in 1978, together with Haruomi Hosono and Yukihiro Takahashi, he started the Yellow Magic Orchestra, one of the world's most influential and innovative groups in electronic music. Pioneers in the use of synthesizers, samplers, sequencers, drum machines, computers, and digital recording technology, they anticipated the "electropop boom" of the 1980s, playing a key role in the de-

Yasuharu Konishi (left) and Maki Nomiya (center) of the Pizzicato Five with Dj Towa Tei (right)

velopment of several genres, including synthpop, electro, and techno, while the lyrics of their songs explored various themes, including some of a sociopolitical and subversive nature. As a soloist, Sakamoto has collaborated with many international artists, such as David Sylvian, Carsten Nicolai, Youssou N'Dour, and Fennesz, composed music for the opening ceremony of the 1992 Barcelona Olympics, and worked on several soundtracks that have won him numerous awards, including an Oscar. His composition "Energy Flow" (1999) was

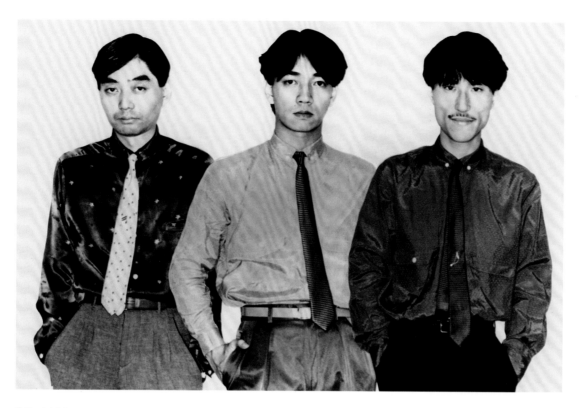

《 Ryuichi Sakamoto (left) and
David Sylvian (right) in Tokyo

⌒ Yellow Magic Orchestra

the first instrumental single to reach No. 1 in the history of Japan's Oricon charts.

Tokyo's music scene is deeply tied to its iconic venues. *Wasei eigo* ("live houses"), very small venues and bars where rock, jazz, blues, and folk music can be heard, have played a crucial role in shaping the city's musical identity. From legendary venues such as Liquidroom and Zepp Tokyo to more intimate settings such as Shinjuku Loft and Shimokitazawa Basement Bar, these clubs over the years have supported many artists and fostered creative communities, continuing to provide space for new sounds in the city.

1912 Students from Tokyo Music School found Hatano Jazz Band, Japan's first jazz ensemble.

1966 The Beatles are the first foreign rock band to play in Japan. The government deploys riot police against young fans outside the Budokan, the arena hosting the show.

1953 Tennessee, the first Western music venue for not just jazz, opens in Ginza.

1958 In February, at Nichigeki's first "Western Carnival," forty-five thousand people watch Japanese rock singers perform.

1978 The Yellow Magic Orchestra is formed.

Zeebra introduces hip-hop to mainstream Japanese music with the single "Mr. Dynamite." **2000**

City pop, inspired by Western lifestyles, becomes one of the most successful genres thanks to artists such as Tatsuro Yamashita and Toshiki Kadomatsu. **1983**

In the growing market of downloadable cell phone ringtones, "Flavor of Life" by Hikaru Utada is the first song in the world to sell more than ten million digital copies in one year. **2008**

Visual kei, a movement characterized by male groups wearing androgynous makeup, hairstyles, and costumes, emerges as a new rock trend. **1990**

About 486,000 people attend Momoiro Clover Z's live shows, the highest attendance for concerts by a female music group in Japan. **2014**

Map of Tokyo

1 Liquidroom
3 Chome-16-6 Higashi, Shibuya City.

2 The Waseda International House of Literature (The Haruki Murakami Library)
169-0051 Tokyo, Shinjuku City, Nishiwaseda, 1 Chome−6.
In the 1970s, writer Haruki Murakami ran a jazz club with his wife. Now his record collection, along with his manuscripts and archive, can be consulted in this library on the Tokyo University campus.

3 Shinjuku Loft
Tatehana Bldg B2F, 1-12-9 Kabuki-cho, Shinjuku-ku.

4 Shimokitazawa Basement Bar
5 Chome-18-1 Daizawa, Setagaya City.

5 The Budokan
2-3 Kitanomaru-koen, Chiyoda City.
An arena initially built for the 1964 Olympics, it later became a temple of music. The Beatles, Bob Dylan, Blur, Pearl Jam, the Modern Jazz Quartet, and many others have played there.

6 Antiknock
160-0022 Tokyo, Shinjuku City, Shinjuku, 4 Chome−3−15.
Since 1985, Antiknock's legendary basement has hosted the best punk and metal live shows in town.

7 Live House Fever
156-0042 Tokyo, Setagaya City, Hanegi, 1 Chome−1−14.
Live house famous for underground shows, standing room only.

8 Eggman
150-0041 Tokyo, Shibuya City, Jinnan, 1 Chome−6−8 B1.
Nights on the Eggman's iconic oval dance floor are the ones that most helped shape the city's J-pop sound.

9 Earthdom
2 Chome-32-3 Okubo, Shinjuku City.
The beating heart of Tokyo's punk and hardcore scene is hard to find because of poor signage, but its stairways covered with shreds of concert flyers are now an institution worth seeking out.

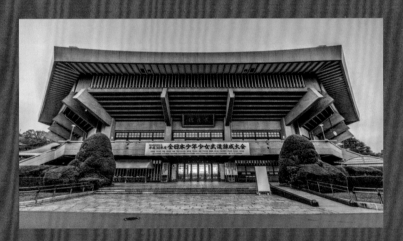
The Budokan

GUIA CORTASSA

Guia is an author, editor, and translator.
She writes about music, literature, and travel
for numerous magazines, especially
international ones, including *The Quietus*,
Loud and Quiet, *Esquire*, and *Mousse*.
She is a speaker, author, and musical selector
at Radio Raheem and is the author
of the successful book *Måneskin.*
Il rock siamo noi.

Credits

WS whitestar™ is a trademark property of White Star s.r.l.

© 2024 White Star s.r.l.
Piazzale Luigi Cadorna, 6
20123 Milan, Italy
www.whitestar.it

Translation: Alexa Ahern for Bianco Tangerine
Editing: Andrea Modica

ISBN 978-88-544-2080-9
1 2 3 4 5 6   28 27 26 25 24

Printed in China